Sisters and Little Saints

Carol Cornwall Madsen
Susan Staker Oman

Sisters and Little Saints

One Hundred Years of Primary

Salt Lake City, Utah
Deseret Book Company
1979

Library of Congress Cataloging in Publication Data

Madsen, Carol Cornwall, 1930-
    Sisters and little saints.

    Includes bibliographical references and index.
    1.   Church of Jesus Christ of Latter-day Saints.
Primary Association—History.   I.   Oman, Susan Staker,
1947-   joint author.   II.   Title.
BX8603.P743M32   267'.7   79-20354
ISBN   0-87747-760-4

Contents

Foreword by
LaVern Watts Parmley

When the Primary Association of The Church of Jesus Christ of Latter-day Saints was founded in 1878, it became the third in a trio of auxiliaries organized and administered by Mormon women. The first two, the Relief Society for women and the Young Ladies' Mutual Improvement Association for older girls, functioned for nearly a decade before the women focused their attention on collectively mothering Zion's children. It was soon apparent that these three organizations, in connection with priesthood quorums and the Sunday School, provided the means whereby "every one from early childhood to maturity, can be led forward step by step, from one degree of knowledge to another until fully qualified to discharge all the duties of perfected and honorable manhood and womanhood." (General Epistle from the Council of the Twelve, 1887.)

The last to be born, the Primary Association was nevertheless the first to write its history. Aurelia Spencer Rogers's *Life Sketches of Orson Spencer and Others, and History of Primary Work,* the founder's own account of Primary beginnings, was published in 1897 upon celebration of the Pioneer Jubilee, barely twenty years after the first Primary Association convened in Farmington, Utah. In the years that followed, the Young Women's Mutual Improvement Association published three and the Relief Society two book-length histories of their organizations. But Sister Rogers's book remained the only source for Primary history. Part of the reason was that for more than half a century the Primary leadership personified the organization's history. Louie B. Felt, called as the Primary's first general president in 1880, served in that capacity until 1925. May Anderson, Louie's close associate, was involved in Primary work from about 1889 until her own term as general president ended in 1940. During these years the Church was small enough and sufficiently Utah-centered that Primary history lessons in the *Children's Friend* sometimes suggested that interested groups make arrangements to call upon Sisters Rogers, Felt, and Anderson in their homes. In other words, Primary history was only "a few doors down."

By the time my service as Primary president ended in 1974, the history of the Primary was somewhat more removed from its hundreds of thousands of children and teachers scattered world-wide. But I had known personally all the Primary presidents who preceded me, except for Louie Felt. My thirty-two years in the general presidency of the Primary had given me a fairly good grasp of its history, so after my release I turned my attention toward compiling this history. My efforts dovetailed with the interests of Leonard J. Arrington, director of the Church Historical Department's History Division, who wanted to undertake a series of oral history interviews with me to help document Primary history. Under his direction Jill Mulvay Derr, research historian within the division, began eight taped interviews covering my personal involvement in the organization.

But there was reason to reach beyond my own administration and also to find the history not included in Sister Rogers's account. How had the Primary Association developed over what was now almost a century? Dr. Arrington suggested that the History Division support me in this enterprise, with the idea that the work could eventually lead to a much-needed book-length study of the Primary's first one hundred years.

Assigned to assist me, Sister Derr helped me through old minute books and long-unturned pages of the *Woman's Exponent,* where we uncovered accounts of the first Primary meetings and fairs. We found Eliza Snow's old "speakers" for Primary children, which included dialogues and recitations that we were sure would never interest today's Primary children. It was delightful to see what they had done for lessons then, since I had always wondered what sisters had used before the *Children's Friend* was published in 1902. The available material mounted. I labeled large manila envelopes and tucked away appropriate photocopies from the *Woman's Exponent* and the *Children's Friend*. Disclaiming my own abilities as a historian, I turned my materials over to Dr. Arrington and offered whatever assistance I could render to complete a history of the Primary as it observed its centennial in 1978.

The History Division began further Primary research. Research fellows, including John McCormick, Collette Maxwell, and Susan Oman, delved into various aspects of the Primary's hundred years. Sister Derr used these materials and the original files in preparing an overview of Primary history, "Sisters and Little Saints," for a Charles Redd Center for Western Studies lecture in spring 1978. The title was so appropriate that it seemed the book-length study could go by no other name.

The task of writing the book on Primary history fell to Carol Cornwall Madsen, a research historian with the division, and research fellow Susan Oman. Their work draws from a multitude of published works and countless archival sources housed in the Church Historical Department. They acknowledge the full support and cooperation of President Naomi M. Shumway and general board members in preparing the final manuscript, with particular thanks to Trilba Lindsay and Janice Piccolo, secretaries of the Primary board.

And so, as this history of the Primary Association goes to press, I express my thanks to Jill Mulvay Derr, Carol Cornwall Madsen, Susan Staker Oman, the Historical Department of the Church, and all others who have helped bring this labor to fruition.

Foreword by
Naomi M. Shumway

The Primary is a unique children's organization that was born in answer to the sincere, searching prayers of a humble handmaiden of the Lord, Aurelia Spencer Rogers. Sister Rogers's heart was drawn to the children of the little community of Farmington, Utah, as she watched their daily activities. She sensed so strongly the need for each child to be taught the gospel of Jesus Christ that she sought for and obtained divine guidance. Heeding the whisperings of the Holy Spirit, she asked, "Could there not be an organization for little boys wherein they could be taught everything good, and how to behave?" She voiced her concern to Eliza R. Snow at a stake Relief Society conference, and she in turn spoke to President John Taylor. After prayerful consideration, and under the direction of the priesthood, the first Primary was organized with Sister Rogers as the president. On August 25, 1878, the first Primary meeting was held in Farmington, where a large group of boys and girls met in a little rock church to be taught obedience, faith in God, prayer, punctuality, and good manners.

In her journal Sister Rogers recorded her feelings about that first Primary day: "It would be impossible for one who had never experienced anything of the kind, to imagine our feelings as we stood before an audience of children who had come there to receive instructions from us. We were very weak indeed, but felt to lean upon the Lord in all humility." The history of Primary had begun.

During one hundred years of Primary thousands of sisters have "leaned upon the Lord in all humility" as they have blessed the lives of the children. Primary teachers are very significant in the lives of the children entrusted to their care. These tender little ones so recently departed from the divine presence of a loving Heavenly Father are choice in his sight. Primary sisters help build the foundation for sound social, emotional, and spiritual development in every child. These truths are reflected in the inspired writings of an ancient prophet: "Train up a child in the way he should go: and when he is old, he will not depart from it." (Proverbs 22:6.) The purpose of the Primary follows the inspiration of the Lord as Primary sisters form a partnership with parents to "teach their children to pray, and to walk uprightly before the Lord." (D&C 68:28.) It has always been the prayer of Primary sisters that each child will learn that he has a Father in heaven who loves him, that each child will know that he can communicate with his Father in heaven through prayer, that each child will come to understand the principles of the gospel and know of the things that are right, and that each child will gain the spiritual strength to face the challenges of each day.

Many have attempted to capture in print the history of the Primary. We are indebted to Carol C. Madsen and Susan S. Oman for their compilation of the research, minutes, and many journals of the Primary organization. They have written an epic portrayal of the love and devotion of Primary sisters for the children and their dedication and willingness to serve their Father in heaven. *Sisters and Little Saints* is not only a tribute to the first one hundred years of Primary, but also a prologue to the future history of Primary, as loving Primary workers will continue to teach the children throughout the world the truths of the gospel of Jesus Christ so they may enjoy the promise of the Lord: "And all thy children shall be taught of the Lord; and great shall be the peace of thy children." (Isaiah 54:13.)

Preface

In 1881 thirteen-year-old Joseph Welch, a member and secretary of the Primary Association of The Church of Jesus Christ of Latter-day Saints in Morgan, Utah, wrote a letter to Eliza R. Snow. She was so impressed with its well-expressed and carefully written ideas that she had it printed in the *Woman's Exponent,* a newspaper published by and for Latter-day Saint women. In the letter Joseph described the success of the new Primary organization in his ward and the "splendid" Primary Fair held in East Porterville, where the boys displayed their handmade rakes, knives, forks, rolling pins, and ox-yokes, and the girls exhibited the pies, cakes, and "tidies" that they had made especially for the fair. "Sister Porter, the President, takes great pains with the children," Joseph continued. "She teaches them to sing, and at the Fair they sang very sweetly. I hope you will be permitted to come and visit us again next summer, for the Primary children would like to see you now."[1]

The next year Joseph was privileged to serve as Primary secretary under his mother, Harriet Nash Welch, who was appointed ward Primary president in 1882. She was already serving as stake Primary president, and filled both assignments until her death in 1894. Older Primary children were often chosen to be secretaries, and mother-child combinations as officers occurred frequently in the early Primaries. Harriet Welch, the mother of nine and foster mother of three, made her mark among the children of Morgan. "No person was more beloved of children than this woman," her biographer reported, "and when she died she was literally buried in a grave of flowers that children and grown folks had brought from all over the Morgan Stake."[2]

The history of the Primary Association is the story of dedicated sisters like Harriet Welch, each striving to teach and train the little Saints. The Primary was established in August 1878 for "disciplining, educating and spiritually cultivating children," and the women of the Church were given the responsibility to organize and administer the new program. As Harriet Welch ably proved, it was a fitting stewardship.

Long before Aurelia Rogers visited with Eliza R. Snow and Emmeline Wells in her parlor in the summer of 1878 and expressed her concern for the unruly behavior of the little boys in Farmington, Mormon mothers had been admonished repeatedly by Church leaders to "look after their children" and teach them "every principle of goodness and virtue." With husbands and fathers engaged in the work of the kingdom, Brigham Young asked the sisters "to act as father and mother to the [children] until they were out of their care. It was their right," he told them, when acting by the power of the priesthood, "to direct the child until it is of a proper age" when it could then be governed by the father and meet its own responsibilities in the kingdom.[3] A decade later Wilford Woodruff repeated the injunction. "Upon the shoulders of you mothers," he told the women assembled in general conference, "rests, in a great measure, the responsibility of correctly developing the mental and moral powers of the rising generation, whether in infancy, childhood, or still riper years.... Our children should be prepared to build up the kingdom of God. Then qualify them in the days of childhood for the great duties they will be called upon to perform."[4]

With such specific admonition it is no wonder that the faithful mothers a century ago were willing to extend their familial and nurturing capacities beyond the circle of their own homes into the entire religious community. They had been told—and it was their conviction that they best knew how—to teach the children of Zion, and they accepted the responsibility to do so.

By 1878 Mormon women had already enjoyed more than a decade of administrative experience in other Church programs, and to take on another organization was merely to expand their sphere of interest and influence. In 1867 the Relief Society of The Church of Jesus Christ of Latter-day Saints was formally reorganized, and local units were established throughout the territory by Eliza R. Snow under the direction of Brigham Young. Two years later, again at the behest of President Young, Sister Snow organized "Retrenchment Associations" (later known as the Young Ladies' and then Young Women's Mutual Improvement Association), which were formed to build testimonies in young women and teach them habits of frugality and moderation. Both organizations assisted the sick and the poor and donated to such worthy projects as temple building, the emigration of needy converts, and the Deseret Hospital. They also participated in the self-sustaining home economy program initiated by Brigham Young by manufacturing silk, making useful commodities of straw, and maintaining women's commission stores to sell their handmade products.

When the Primary was organized its members participated in these activities as well as in projects of benevolent service, another function of the Relief Society. By extending their own programs and interests into the Retrenchment and Primary Associations, Relief Society sisters involved the younger women and children in those projects that had become their responsibility. Studying the gospel, learning to speak in public, contributing to the economy of the kingdom, and alleviating the needs of the poor were deemed steps as valuable in developing little Saints as in making older ones. As late as 1890, one stake president said the three women's organizations—the Relief Society, the Young Women's Mutual Improvement Association, and the Primary—"are all so closely connected that I could not tell where one begins and the other ends." He called the women "Sisters of Charity."[5]

In the granting of suffrage to Utah women in 1870, the publication of the *Woman's Exponent,* beginning in 1872, and the call for women to study medicine in 1873, Mormon women found additional opportunities to meet the mandate given to them to "look after the children." Emmeline B. Wells, fifth general president of the Relief Society and fervent suffragist, argued that the ballot in woman's hands would enable her "to exert an instrumentality in all departments whereby her offspring could be protected, educated and provided for."[6] She encouraged women in all states and territories that permitted it to exercise their franchise "for all measures for the suppressing of vice and immorality of every sort, that the children and youth...may be protected by law."[7]

Sister Wells had reason to encourage Mormon sisters to use every means available to protect their youth from unhealthy influences. In 1880, only two years after the organization of the Primary, the census showed that 44 percent of Utah's population were under the age of fourteen and another 10 percent were between ages fifteen and nineteen. Having an imperfect school system and few recreational opportunities, and being a decade or two past the unremitting work of frontier days, the Great Basin region offered its numerous youth increasing leisure time but little to do with it. As early as 1861 Brigham Young was concerned with the problem of restless teenagers. He favored the construction of social and recreational halls in each ward to provide recreation for youth "who would otherwise meet in small groups and indulge in low, grovelling rowdyism." In 1874 the *Deseret News* printed an appeal from public authorities: "Parents, why do you allow your children to be out so much at night after dark? They there and then learn many things which they would not at home and which are nothing to their benefit.... Just look after these little ones, and have self interest enough not to forget the proverb about 'as the twig is bent,' etc."[8]

The *Woman's Exponent* also expressed concern for Zion's children. One contributor in 1873 advised mothers to cling to their children and not "send them out from you, to see, hear and learn all the evils that prevail in this fast age, before their minds are capable of comprehending right from wrong."[9] Another asked, "Do we mothers teach our children as we ought?" She had suggested to a son not to pick the peaches until they were ripe, but was answered by another family member, "If he does not pick them, the neighbor's boys will; for ever since the apricots began to ripen, they have run through the orchard, climbed the trees, and pelted each other with the fruit."[10]

Clearly, there was concern for the conduct of the future leaders of the kingdom, and the *Exponent* filled its columns with advice to mothers on setting good examples for their children and teaching them proper behavior. It counseled young women to consider fully and wisely the responsibilities of motherhood, warning them of the importance of "the early training of the little ones,...for Motherhood," it regretfully reported, "is a vocation in which more women fail than in any other."[11]

Another major concern of women was the health and physical well-being of their children. While Utah's infant mortality rate did not exceed the national average, Church leaders recognized the need for better medical service in the growing territory. Disease, accident, and the normal hazards of childbirth took a heavy toll of the little Saints. In August 1873, at the suggestion of Brigham Young, Eliza R. Snow issued a call to women to study medicine either at home or away in order to become midwives, nurses, and even doctors.[12] Several women left home and family for three or four years in order to receive medical degrees from accredited eastern colleges, returning home to put their training to work in behalf of their people. Ellis Reynolds Shipp, one of the faithful women who answered the call to study medicine, traveled all the way to Philadelphia to attend a woman's medical college. "This separation is oh, so trying to my 'Mother heart,'" she noted in her diary, "but I am willing to suffer myself if I can thereby increase and improve the advantages of my dear children."[13] When Dr. Shipp returned to Salt Lake City she taught medicine to hundreds of women throughout the territory who utilized their training to assist women in childbirth and children in sickness.[14]

The sacrifice of these women to study medicine was but another manifestation of the willingness of Mormon women generally to give of themselves in behalf of their children. The Primary Association was a natural outgrowth of this maternal concern, and offered women the opportunity to extend their active caring to all children.

Like the other Church auxiliaries, the Primary was organized in response to a need. By 1878 the time was ripe for the little Saints to feel the full impact of the collective concern of the mothers of Israel. Their undirected energies would now be harnessed by capable and inspired women, willing to meet the charge to "fit and qualify...and train" Zion's children "to look forward to the destiny that God has in store for them." The special nature of the call to reach the children of the Church found worthy expression in the words of Elder Franklin D. Richards of the Council of the Twelve and could well reflect the devotion of thousands of women who have accepted that call during the last hundred years. In 1885 he admonished the Saints of Ogden to try to understand more perfectly the worth of souls. "Oh, if the sisters and brethren that have the charge of these little Primary Associations could only realize that every little child is a gem that they are called upon to polish, to cut, to refine, to shape, to burnish, to fit and prepare to stand in the diadem of its Father's crown," he said. "This is the way in which we ought to look at these small but precious jewels."[15]

Carol C. Madsen
Susan S. Oman

Sisters and Little Saints

Mural depicting first Primary meeting, Farmington (Utah) Ward chapel

Chapter 1

"Could There Not Be an Organization?"

The train to Salt Lake City was not due for some time. To escape the summer heat, Eliza R. Snow and Emmeline B. Wells, in company with several other sisters who had attended the Relief Society conference in Farmington, Utah, stopped at the home of Aurelia Spencer Rogers. The conversation turned to young people, especially "the rough, careless ways many of the young men and boys had at the time." "What will our girls do for good husbands, if this state of things continues?" queried Aurelia, who had been privately considering such questions for some months. Since Eliza seemed particularly impressed with the question, Aurelia continued: "Could there not be an organization for little boys, and have them trained to make better men?"[1] Thus that summer day in 1878 were the wheels set in motion that would lead to the establishment of a Primary Association for Latter-day Saint children, the first meeting of which would be held in Farmington that fall under Sister Rogers's direction.

It was not surprising that the conversation had turned to children. Eliza had been a teacher and a writer of children's stories and poems, and Aurelia had been mothering for more than thirty years. The meeting that day was merely the catalyst needed to spark Aurelia's motherly commitment to a specific course of action and to enlist Eliza's prodigious gifts in the service of Zion's young.

Aurelia came by her concern for children through a long apprenticeship in mothering. At twelve years of age she, along with her fourteen-year-old sister Ellen, had assumed the care of four younger brothers and sisters when their mother died in the flight from Nauvoo, Illinois, during the winter of 1846. The next two years in Winter Quarters and the following year in the Salt Lake Valley had found the motherless family also temporarily fatherless when their father, Orson Spencer, was called on a proselyting mission to Great Britain. Learning from the trying experience, Aurelia felt that she had a natural proclivity for the young.

Two years after her father's return from his mission, Aurelia married young Thomas Rogers, whom she had met crossing the plains in Brigham Young's company. By her eighteenth birthday the next year, 1852, Aurelia had given birth to her first son. In the next two decades she would bear twelve children, losing five of them in early childhood. In 1871 she buried her third child in succession, and grieved bitterly: "It seemed indeed as if my last hope was gone.... And I almost lost faith in God; for once in my life, I even doubted the existence of a Supreme Being." But an encouraging letter from her father from many years before came to her mind, telling her to trust in God "though he slay you"; and after fervent prayer asking for forgiveness for her wavering faith, she pledged her trust "henceforth and forever."[2]

The son and daughter born in 1873 and 1874, after five little ones had been lost, were particularly dear to her, and her commitment to the children of Zion no doubt was forged by these trying personal experiences.

While Aurelia was rearing her family, Eliza R. Snow was contributing songs, poems, and stories to the Sunday School's *Juvenile Instructor,* a semimonthly newspaper for children and their teachers. Commenting on bad words, current styles, and the evils of candy, she also wrote a series of Bible stories and answered the letters of children who for a variety of reasons had written to her. "You say, 'I want to grow up to be useful in the kingdom of God,'" she wrote one little namesake. "You could not have written anything that would please me better."[3] When she accompanied her brother, Lorenzo Snow, and other Church officials on a tour of Europe and Palestine in 1872-73, she sent letters to the magazine, describing children's schools that she had visited: an "object school" in Paris and a kindergarten in Munich. She described the children's lunches and their marching, singing, and crafts, and commented on their "robust" health. "Not only the poor," she wrote to editor George Q. Cannon, "but many wealthy parents avail themselves of having their little ones kindly cared for and trained by these skillful matrons."[4] Though childless herself, Sister Snow had consistently shown a sincere interest in the young.

Before their meeting in Aurelia's Farmington parlor that summer of 1878, both women had been contemplating the problems facing the generation of young people who had never known the trials and persecutions of founding and colonizing. Bishop John W. Hess of the Farmington Ward had called the mothers together almost a year before to consider the challenge. At that meeting he had told the women it was their responsibility to train and guide the young minds of children. Aurelia felt that such training required the united efforts of the parents; and knowing that some in the community were careless of that duty, she considered going to the YMMIA to talk about the problem. But a natural shyness and concern for what others would think kept her from acting on the impulse.

Though Aurelia did not follow her initial impulse, she did continue to ponder the challenge issued by her bishop. "I was always an earnest thinker, and naturally of a religious turn of mind," she recalled, "...and for some time...I had reflected seriously upon the necessity of more strict discipline for our little boys." Nothing, she reflected, not the careless attitude of the times or the difficult circumstances the Mormons had endured, "should...be allowed to come before the most sacred duty of parentage, that of looking after the spiritual welfare of the children."[5]

While Aurelia struggled to find an answer to her problem, Eliza was reflecting on the same concern. In January 1878 she visited the Seventeenth Ward in Salt Lake City to organize a Young Ladies' Mutual Improvement Association. She spoke of a Juvenile Society organized spontaneously by some very young girls in the ward about four years before.

In lauding these girls for their initiative, she articulated this concern:

> When we first came here there were no regular schools; but as soon as we obtained the necessaries of life, attention was turned to educating the children mentally, but as they were born in the Church, and heirs by right to the kingdom, no thought was bestowed upon their spiritual culture.
>
> The world educate their children to the highest mental standpoint within their reach. But we had come out of Babylon, and thought we had left her behind; but the spirit of the world had crept in among our young people, and we had Infidels among them, children of good parents; and the question was asked, "What will become of our children?"[6]

Both women, then, each with a different background and perspective, had considered the spiritual welfare of the children of the Saints, and Aurelia's question, "Could there not be an organization?" was particularly timely.

Eliza R. Snow was an auspicious partner in the Primary's beginning because by 1878 she was not only president of the Relief Society, but also an expert in Church administrative procedures, the acknowledged leader of Mormon women. Her first experience in organization had come three decades before, in 1842, when the Relief Society was organized in Nauvoo and she was appointed secretary. Designated "Zion's Poetess" by the Prophet Joseph Smith, she occupied a prominent position even then among the women of the Church. After the Prophet's death and in the years that followed at Winter Quarters, across the plains, and in early Great Salt Lake City, she emerged as the spiritual and intellectual leader of Mormon women. The Relief Society had been discontinued since the exodus from Nauvoo, so she assumed no formal leadership until 1867, when Brigham Young gave her instructions to organize Female Relief Societies throughout the territory and instructed bishops to support her. With this assignment she functioned as an auxiliary adviser to President Young regarding the expanding concerns of women. In the late 1860s she also became his representative in organizing "Young Ladies' Retrenchment Associations," forerunners of the Young Ladies' Mutual Improvement Association. It was therefore natural for her to assume a principal leadership role in founding an organization for the younger children as well.

Eliza Snow knew that a critical first step in any undertaking within the Church was obtaining priesthood authorization. After securing the approbation of John Taylor, president of the Council of the Twelve and presiding officer of the Church in 1878, a year after the death of Brigham Young, she took the next important steps. She wrote Bishop Hess for permission to organize the Primary in his ward and received the permission along with his blessing. She then told Sister Rogers that "she [Aurelia] might consider herself authorized to proceed," which she did, while Eliza organized a Primary in the Eleventh Ward in Salt Lake City.[7]

With Eliza's assurance and a calling from her bishop, Aurelia began the work of organizing the first meeting of the new children's association. No mention of girls had been made up to that point, but since "singing was necessary," Aurelia felt that girls should be included in the new organization "to make it sound as well as it should."[8] Accordingly, she wrote a letter to Eliza requesting her opinion, and received a very encouraging letter dated August 4, 1878: "The spirit and contents of your letter pleased me much. I feel assured that the inspiration of heaven is directing you, and that a great and very important movement is being inagurated for the future of Zion." Eliza again emphasized that the priesthood fully supported the movement: "President John Taylor fully approbates it, and Joseph F. Smith thinks we might better afford what expense might be incurred in furnishing uniforms, musical instruments, etc., for the cultivation of the children in Zion, than what we are expending in converting people abroad where elders spend years in converting a very few."[9]

In the same letter she wrote that she had already discussed the idea with a sister in a Salt Lake ward and added, "The importance of the movement, and its great necessity is fully acknowledged by all with whom I have conversed on the subject."

In addition to the encouragement of Eliza Snow and the approval of the priesthood leaders, Sister Rogers received a personal spiritual assurance as well:

> While thinking over what has to be done for the best good of the children, I seemed to be carried away in the spirit, or at least I experienced a feeling of untold happiness which lasted three days and nights. During that time nothing could worry or irritate me; if my little ones were fretful, or the work went wrong, I had patience, could control in kindness, and manage my household affairs easily. This was a testimony to me that what was being done was from God.[10]

On Sunday, August 11, 1878, an organizational meeting was held for the Primary Mutual Improvement Association, a name suggested by Eliza and shortened before long to Primary Association. Aurelia and counselors Louisa Haight and Helen Miller were sustained and set apart. Aurelia then spoke to the group:

> I feel that this move will be of much benefit. When little children pray it will avail much. While they are running loose, the Adversary will feel that he can instill into their tender minds such influences that in their youth will make them subject to him. But I feel that in this he will be baffled....
>
> In this association Children will be taught that one child is no better than another only as it does better, if one has *more* ability, it is no better than another that with more *labour can do less*....Not by the number of Talents, but by the use we make of them are we judged. The strong should help the weak, and make *them* feel that they can do something—my intentions are to speak and act with the Spirit of the Lord.[11]

Bishop Hess also spoke, explaining that he was calling the sisters together for the purpose of asking them "to exercise their influence in their spheres":

> As soon as the Brethren are at home I intend to call them together. There are excesses and evils that need correcting. I

with others have been called to mourn over the looseness, the midnight walk of the Streets &c. &c. I feel the weight of these things, and want the Brethren and the Sisters to each do their part in correcting them. If I had the power I would throw around our young people a shield that would preserve them from the *Evil One,* but we must not be too enthusiastic, it is only the steady advance that will be lasting. The success of this movement depends much upon the influence and efforts of the Mothers.[12]

At the suggestion of the bishop, Aurelia and her counselors visited every house in the ward during the next two weeks, taking the name and age of each child, a total of 224 children. The day appointed for the meeting was Sunday, August 25. One can imagine the scene of that first Primary! What was in the heart of Aurelia Rogers as she stood in the meetinghouse, watching the children trooping into the chapel and taking their place in history? Now that they were finally brought together in an organization of their own and sitting there before her, what should she say to them and what should she do? She evidently felt that order was the first item of business, and so after the opening prayer she organized the children into age groups with the oldest child in each group serving as monitor. This division was for the purpose of order only, since all of the children would meet together in each Primary for at least another decade until the Primaries were graded. Then, probably attacking one of the most irritating problems she had observed, she instructed the little boys not to go into orchards and melon patches that were not their own, and told the little girls not to hang on to wagons, a practice not only wrong but also danger- ous. After a few more admonitions to the children to be obedient to their parents and teachers and kind to one another, the meeting was adjourned until Saturday, September 7, at three in the after- noon. Aurelia's appraisal of this first historic meeting was a little less than wholly enthusiastic. "It was not quite a success," she felt, "on account of unforeseen hindrances and some of the children not knowing the hour of meeting."[13] Her anticipation of the long- dreamed-for occasion undoubtedly left her vulnerable to minor

7

disappointments, but the perpetuation of the organization is the greatest evidence of the success of that first meeting.

Fourteen years later Aurelia Rogers would learn personally of the success of her Primary. On the evening of June 24, 1892, several of the original children of that first Primary meeting, then grown to womanhood and manhood, drove up to her home in their horse-drawn buggies. They were accompanied by members of the ward bishopric and the two counselors of the stake presidency, one of whom was former bishop John W. Hess. The group had come to escort Sister Rogers and her family to the wardhouse, where a dinner and program in her honor awaited her. The room, adorned with flowers, was filled with friends. Tributes were read, and songs written to commemorate the occasion were sung. One essay, written and read by former Farmington Primary girl Anna Clark Tanner, bespeaks the impact of the Primary on the lives of its first members and many children since:

> As children, we were proud to have our own little meetings, for even then did we know that the interesting stories and encouraging words of Sister Rogers and her co-laborers made it easier for us to be obedient, to resist temptation, control our tempers, and keep the Sabbath day holy....
>
> Who of us have forgotten the impressive lessons taught us on the Word of Wisdom?...How many of us received our first lesson in singing in the Primary Association, and with what pride did the little boys, dressed in uniform, show their skill in playing the flute, etc.? No one will forget the first carpet made by the patient fingers of the little Primary girls. And the lessons of industry that were taught us in the bean patch will long be remembered with pride and pleasure. The concerts and fairs were our delight. What a broad field of usefulness was presented to us....
>
> I think that I speak for all faithful members of the Primary when I say that much of our happiness and prosperity, and ambition to become good and useful, is due to the valuable instructions and encouragement received in the Primary Association.[14]

A week before the first meeting in Farmington, Eliza R. Snow was in Ogden presiding at a conference of the Relief Society and Young Ladies' Mutual Improvement Association. She was already laying the groundwork for the Primary there. She spoke to the women about the disciplining and educating of children, particularly their spiritual cultivation, and told them of a plan to "inaugurate a system of Primary Associations." She also lamented the lack among children of the spiritual gifts that had been manifested in the early days of the Church. A special organizational meeting was called for little children and their parents the next morning, Saturday, August 17, 1878. Sister Snow also spoke to this gathering, at which three hundred children recorded their intent to become members of the proposed Primary Association.[15]

Returning to Salt Lake City, Eliza spoke to a group of Relief Society women and reported her activities in the northern part of the territory during the preceding month. Primary presidents and counselors had been set apart in most of the wards of Box Elder Stake and a special children's meeting had been called like the one in Ogden. "I told [the children] it was their meeting, to worship God," she reported. "They sang standing and prayed kneeling. They paid good attention to all they could understand. They expressed themselves glad to have an organization of their own, so they would not be afraid to speak." Then she challenged the women: "I would like to know how many in this congregation are willing to unite with us and sustain the Primary Associations here." On motion all present rose to their feet. "Thank you, sisters," continued Eliza, "we will have it. We want to take the hearts of the young while they can be impressed."[16]

She then nominated a twenty-eight-year-old woman, Louie Bouton Felt, to preside over a Primary Association in the Eleventh Ward in Salt Lake City. The first meeting of that ward Primary, the second in the Church to convene, was attended by Eliza and her counselor in the Relief Society, Zina D. H. Young. At a conference of the Relief Societies of the Salt Lake Stake a week later, three more ward Primary presidencies were sustained. Under Eliza's experienced direction, the Primary Association had begun to spread throughout the territory before the fledgling Farmington group was a month old.

During the next months and years, Relief Society leaders from Salt Lake City, under the direction of Sister Snow, continued to assume the major role in organizing Primary Associations throughout the territory. Joseph Smith had "turned the key" for women through the Relief Society organization in the early days of the Church, and, under the direction of Brigham Young, the women had gradually assumed many collective responsibilities in building the dreamed-of kingdom of God. Among these collective responsibilities, as Bishop Hess explained to the women of Farmington, was the responsibility to extend their mothering role outside the home into the Church community. Through the Young Women's MIA and the Primary Associations the women met this assignment, as another bishop defined it, to "teach our young people, and also the children how to conduct themselves in a proper manner under every condition and circumstance of life."[17]

A mother-daughter relationship among the women's auxiliaries of the Church was expressed procedurally by the fact that Relief Society leaders could organize Young Women's Mutual Improvement Associations and, later, Primary Associations without priesthood assistance, though priesthood approval was necessary. Eliza R. Snow was given additional authority to set apart the Primary presidents she called to serve in the wards and stakes. Organizing or reorganizing Relief Societies, however, required not only priesthood approval, but also priesthood participation.

Relief Society leaders had the responsibility to organize Primaries throughout the territory even after a general Primary president was called in 1880. Zina Young, who had attended the first meeting of the Eleventh Ward Primary in Salt Lake City with Sister Snow in September 1878, visited many of the towns in Utah County the following October, attending various women's conferences held conjointly by the Relief Society and Young Women's MIA. While there she organized eight Primary Associations. This coordinated activity of supervising the women's organizations and organizing new Primaries was repeated again and again during the next six years in virtually every village throughout the territory. In one remarkable trip to Southern Utah in the winter of 1880-1881, Eliza, who was then seventy-six years old, and Zina, a mere sixty, traveled over a thousand miles by train and wagon and established thirty-five Primaries, while conducting the business of the other women's auxiliaries and doing temple work in the St. George Temple.

These first meetings were often impressive occasions for those present, especially the children. Sister Snow tried to impress on the young children the importance of these modest beginnings. "In the time of Joseph Smith," she told one Primary, "the children had little meetings and bore testimony and had the good spirit with them."[18] One woman recalled Sister Snow's visit to Cedar City in 1880 to organize a Primary of twenty children:

> During the organization meeting Sister Snow showed us a watch which had been the Prophet Joseph's. She told us about the Prophet and the watch. She let each of us hold the watch for a short time. I remember as I held the watch in my tiny cupped hands, she gave us an admonition not to ever forget that we had held the Prophet's watch. . . . I imagine the rest remembered as I shall always, the story Sister Snow told us of the Prophet and the wonderful moment when we held his watch.[19]

Hundreds of children must have held this watch during the organizing years of the Primary and also remembered vividly those earliest meetings. One eleven-year-old girl from the St. George area, not yet born when Eliza visited her home village the winter of 1880, was nevertheless affected by the often retold story of the memorable event:

> Our president was telling us not long ago of one of our boys who was healed in the primary meeting when it was first organized. Sisters Eliza R. Snow and Zina D. Young were here at the time. This boy was very sick and weak, and had to be carried to meeting. He wanted to be prayed for, so at the

close of the meeting Sister Snow told the children to arise to their feet, close their eyes, and repeat after her the prayer, one sentence at a time. She prayed for the sick boy. When they got through praying he got up, walked home, and got into a wagon without help. He was well from that time.[20]

Wherever she went to visit the Primaries, Sister Snow left vivid impressions on the minds of her youthful listeners, and because of the diligence of the young secretaries who kept records of her sermons, her messages were repeated untold numbers of times with similarly impressionable children taking careful notes. At a conference in Farmington only months after the Primary had been organized there, she told the young saints that she wanted them to pay strict attention, that she had once attended a meeting of five hundred Lamanites and only a few white people, but that the Indians kept the best order. She also told them of the time when seventy-five Indian braves came to see Joseph Smith. "They fixed their eyes upon him and did not move about to get better places as did some of the Whites," she remembered. "Joseph," she continued, "said he wished the Saints would learn manners from the Indians."

How impressed the children must have been to hear her say that holy angels were there among them, taking minutes of what was being done and "bearing a good report up to the people of light, those who have been good here and have died."

She reminded children everywhere of the love the Prophet Joseph had for them, and told the children of Farmington of a time when Joseph had to have a guard day and night to protect him from his enemies who were seeking his life. One evening he overheard children praying in turn, one after another, that his life might be spared. That night he told the guard, "You may go to bed; I am safe for tonight." The children of Farmington learned that Joseph had faith in the prayers of little children.[21]

The significance of the founding of the Primary must have been stamped on the hearts of the children when they heard of the Prophet Joseph's confidence in them, held his watch, and joined their faith with Sister Snow's in prayer for their companions. But Eliza wanted the sacredness and the importance of these events to be equally impressive to the sisters who were called to teach the little ones. She told the sisters that she thought it necessary that "the very best talent in our midst should be employed to preside over the Primary Associations," women who loved children and had "the faculty of drawing them to them."[22] The concern for capable leadership of children was thus manifested in the very beginning and has remained an important priority to the present.

By the mid-1880s a Primary group had been organized by Relief Society officers in nearly every Mormon settlement, and the work of the Primary had been vigorously launched. In many respects the concern of Mormon women for children paralleled the "social housekeeping" efforts of other nineteenth century American women. The Primary came at the same time that Americans in general were demonstrating increased concern for children by giving new emphasis to the medical care of children, considering the enactment of child labor laws, and establishing children's aid societies and institutions for deaf and blind children.

But the contours of the Primary Association, though reflecting common concerns for the welfare of children, would be uniquely Mormon, shaped by the problems as well as the needs of the growing and dynamic institution that the Church had become by 1880. The fledgling Primary was marked indelibly with the vision and insight of two women—Aurelia Spencer Rogers and Eliza R. Snow. Born of the motherly concern of one woman for her own sons and daughters, which she extended to all the children of Zion, the idea for the association found form in the capable hands of a great leader who, though childless herself, felt the same concern. The fortuitous meeting of these two women in a Farmington parlor during the summer of 1878 sparked the beginnings of the Primary, an organization to "convert" the children of Zion to their heritage and to their God.

Early Primary picnic

Chapter 2

"Worthy of All Honor"

"I am now devoting what time I can to a series of three books for the Primary Associations, especially for recitations," wrote Eliza R. Snow on Christmas day 1881 to a young Primary secretary who had reported the activities of his local association in a letter to her. "These books are very much needed, and I feel anxious to get them out as soon as possible, but so much of my time is taken up in other directions that my progress is slow at present."[1]

The previous year Eliza had spent Christmas in the St. George, Utah, area, much of her time devoted to organizing new Primaries there. In spite of her many involvements, a curriculum for the new organization and the observations of her young correspondent were important priorities to her. At the initial meeting of one of these associations in "Mormon Dixie" she had counseled "not to make the meetings a school and become tedious. Have short prayers, speeches, and exercises, and have them in the spirit of the Gospel."[2] Though there would be similarities, Sunday School was not to be the model for the new association. Many Mormon women were teachers in the Sunday School at that time, but it was not their organization. The Primary, on the other hand, conceived and administered by women, would reflect their unique talents and concerns.

The Sunday School had been publishing material for children in the *Juvenile Instructor* since 1866, and in 1879 and 1880 the auxiliary also published two readers, the first and second *Book for Our Little Friends*. In 1882 the organization published a catechism, *Questions and Answers on the Life and Mission of the Prophet Joseph Smith,* and the *Deseret Sunday School Music Book* in 1884. Though

15

such material could be helpful, Eliza felt the Primary children should have their own separate materials. By the time she wrote her letter to the young Primary secretary on Christmas day 1881 she had already prepared a hymnbook, a tune book, and a catechism of Old and New Testament questions and answers specifically for the Primary. She was also at work on a series of books containing recitations and dialogues.

Primaries throughout the territory were soon united by their common use of these books, as noted one appreciative Primary leader from Utah's Sanpete Valley: "Since Sister E.R.S. [Eliza R. Snow] Smith's Primary books have been in use the children's selections have improved, till they are all that could be wished for, while prior to that time, if not guarded against, the selection of songs, recitations, etc., were not always as appropriate as they might be."[3]

Children all over the territory might be heard singing the same songs or answering in unison questions from Sister Snow's catechism:

1Q. How long did Moses stay in the mount?
A. Forty days and forty nights.
2Q. What did God give Moses on the mount?
A. Two tables of stone.
3Q. What were on the tables?
A. Ten commandments.
4Q. What were they written by?
A. The finger of God.
5Q. How did the people feel about Moses staying so long?
A. They wondered what had become of him.
6Q. What did they say to Aaron?
A. "Make us gods to go before us."[4]

Many children memorized a poem on a recurrent theme in all the associations, such as the following, on the Word of Wisdom:

First Child
Cold water! cold water!
O that is the drink!

How strange and how foolish
   That any should think
That whisky or brandy,
   That dram-keepers sell,
Is good as the water
    We get from the well!
     Second Child
Cold water! cold water!
   We draw it today;
'Tis as free as the breezes—
   We drink without pay
It never makes drunkards—
   It's pure as can be;
Oh this is the beverage
   For you and for me.
     Third Child
Cold water! cold water!
   Ye drunkards take heed;
Cold water, cold water,
   Is all that you need
To drink when you're thirsty
   O, drink and be *free!*
Cold water's the beverage
   For you and for me.
     All
Cold water! cold water!
   O that is the drink!
How strange and how foolish
   That any should think
That whisky or brandy,
   That dram-keepers sell,
Is good as the water
   We draw from the well.[5]

    Though children in both the Sunday School and the Primary echoed catechisms, recited poems, and dramatized dialogues—all typical nineteenth century methods of pedagogy—there were some

17

differences between the two organizations beyond the fact that the Sunday School was administered by the priesthood and the Primary by the women. Sunday School was taught much like the nineteenth century schools. In early Utah, Sunday Schools even taught basic reading skills. Both Utah public schools and the Sunday Schools were graded, beginning in the late 1870s and early 1880s, and a typical activity in the individual Sunday School class was "reading 'round."[6] The children would take turns reading from a text, such as the published Sunday School readers, and discussing the material as they went along, an activity that might be duplicated in their weekday schools. "Reading 'round" was never a common Primary activity, for as Eliza R. Snow had maintained, the Primaries were not to be schools in the traditional sense.

In Primary the very young could express themselves to each other. Said one worker, "The little ones [felt] that these were their own meetings."[7] From the beginning Eliza had invited children of all ages to express their feelings in their meetings. Children as well as parents had been invited to the organizational meeting in Ogden on August 17, 1878, at which Eliza presided, and they as well as their parents had been asked to sustain the new movement. In the local associations children were often invited not only to bear their testimonies, but also to express publicly what they liked about Primary. Primary officers, priesthood leaders, and a variety of guests often lectured the children in their meetings, but the bulk of the weekly program was devoted to songs, poems, dialogues, and other activities presented by the children. "Mary Haight and Sarah J. Robinson sang a song, Master Daniel Miller recited 'Restoration of the Gospel,' Leonidas Kennard 'Santa Claus,' and Sophia Clark 'The Rich Farmer's Wife,'" recorded the secretary at the eighth meeting of the pioneer Farmington Primary on October 19, 1878. This pattern was mirrored in Primaries throughout the territory during the next few years. Secretaries recording the events were often children.

Latter-day Saint women had learned the art of public speaking during the 1870s as the Relief Society assumed increasingly public undertakings. Speaking before other women and especially before men for the first time was often a frightening experience for sisters whose chief responsibilities had previously been in the privacy of their homes. It is not surprising that through the next decade they were concerned with the children's ability to speak extemporaneously and to express themselves publicly with dignity and poise.

By the mid-1880s Eliza could report optimistically of the children's growing skills in at least one ward:

We had the proof of the benefits they are securing to themselves before us. The girls efficiently led in singing—one of the boys dismissed the meeting in the forenoon, another made the opening prayer in the afternoon, and another, when asked by the president if he had a recitation prepared, answered in the negative; he then arose and made a very nice extempore speech, which amply atoned for the omission. These boys and girls are preparing themselves for future usefulness and honor.[8]

The goal of "mutual improvement" adopted for the young women and young men in their respective associations applied as appropriately to the young children. Some wards organized bands and choruses, and others sponsored manuscript newspapers written and edited by the children. At least one ward sported an ingenious "Picture Gallery" of pencil drawings to develop the children's artistic skill. They drew pictures of "the president and her counselors, gorillas, monkeys, roosters, cats, geometric lines and solids, pretty rooms, and even fine clothes...."[9] Many children learned to dance, performing in May Day festivals or in other special celebrations, such as Brigham Young's birthday, which was commemorated by the Primaries each June. One woman recalled the dances held in the two-room Relief Society hall in her ward when she was a child:

...a large pot-bellied stove...stood in the northeast corner of the large room.

There was always a dance for the children at Christmas and other holidays. The officers carried wood and coal from their homes when the dances were held in the wintertime. The children danced the Virginia Reel, the Circle Dance, In and Out the Window, and some remember the Shoemaker's Dance.... When dances were held in the winter a Primary officer would stand near the stove to protect the children from getting burned.[10]

The showcase for the children's talents was the annual "entertainment" held in each ward. These programs were as varied as the children's experiences in their local associations. A spectator at one of these events recalled that "the costumes were appropriate and pretty, and the dance of the fairies at the close with colored lights was as lovely a scene as anyone would wish to witness." The production was a "Fairy Drama" with the children dressed up as the Fairy Queen, the Genii, the Earth Child, and Fairies.[11] The Eleventh Ward in Salt Lake City was well known for its successful productions. On New Year's night one year, one hundred twenty-five children sang, presented recitations and dialogues, and dramatized "The Sleeping Beauty" for an appreciative audience, who complimented Sister Felt on the "very creditable affair."[12]

This entertainment in the Eleventh Ward not only exhibited the children's accomplishments, but also cleared forty-one dollars, which was donated to the Deseret Hospital. As part of its program, the Primary Association encouraged the children to contribute to the hospital and to meetinghouses, to the temples, and to the European emigration fund. It was also necessary for the individual Primaries to purchase their own books and pay for costumes or other materials used by the children for their activities. The Relief Society women had learned much about managing their own finances during the previous decade and wanted to pass such lessons on to the children as well. The little Saints, whose donations of nickels and "Sunday eggs" were dutifully recorded in local minute books by conscientious young secretaries, were learning along with their mothers how to earn and manage money and how to give of themselves and their means to the building of the kingdom.

Whereas the women sold the products of their home industry in local Relief Society commission stores and used the money to finance the Society's growing concerns, children sold their handiwork at local Primary fairs and thus helped to finance their own association's needs. In early days, handiwork was not taught in Primary, as it was later, but simply reflected work most children did at home. Displaying the products of the children's work was one way to praise them for their economic contribution to the kingdom, in much the same way the sisters were being praised for their involvement in home industries. "When the day comes that Babylon falls, and we are thrown upon our own resources," wrote one Primary president, "then, if not before, will we likely see the good of these Fairs, that are now almost left for the little ones to monopolize."[13] A report in the *Woman's Exponent* of one Primary Fair in 1882 reflected the scope of the children's involvement. "The house was tastefully decorated with evergreens and vases of flowers and smoke-tree," the article stated, "and hundreds of items were on display: quilts, cushions, mats and curtains; petticoats, garters, lace and pillowslips; wax flowers, wool flowers, cornucopias and hanging baskets; breads, cakes and bottled fruits. The boys' department consisted of wheelbarrows, rakes, shovels, plows, rolling pins and potato mashers. Both boys and girls drew and framed pictures and they embroidered or painted mottoes and maps to put on display."[14]

Since the proceeds from the Primary fairs were used not only to fund the associations but also to assist in the economic programs of the kingdom, the bishops of wards with enterprising Primaries were laudatory of their efforts. "Had the various exhibits been produced by adults," exclaimed one enthusiastic bishop of his ward's Primary fair, "still they would be creditable; they show indeed a bright prospect for home industry when those children come to riper years."[15]

Lest parents and leaders became overzealous in extolling the accomplishments of the children, Aurelia Rogers struck a warning note, no doubt gained from experience:

21

There is danger of dishonesty being thoughtlessly encouraged in these fairs if we do not guard against it. Children are apt to be quite elated over making things to place on exhibition, and many times take the entire credit of doing what some one else has helped them to do. It is not expected that our boys and girls can make all such articles as those previously mentioned without the assistance or instruction of father, mother, or others. Then why not have the truth stated on the label? For instance, "Hay-rack made by John Smith assisted by his father."[16]

The children in some wards raised beans and corn, and gleaned and stored wheat. Others braided yards of carpets for local meeting-houses and for the temples. Children were workers in every aspect of the Primary program, as one young girl recalled:

Our Primary Conference took place on a warm day in July. In preparation we children spent a day cleaning the schoolroom. Henrietta and I were there filling our bucket with water from the ditch and carrying it between us into the room. I recall scrubbing the top of a grimy desk until a tall girl came with a cloth in hand and rinsed the mortar-like substance off and wiped it clean. Walls and ceiling were brushed, window casements were cleaned and the glass panes polished. Our bishop sent a green spray of asparagus from his garden which was placed over each of the three tall windows, which made a pleasing decoration.[17]

Children were thus given the opportunity to participate in many of the kingdom-building activities that were also engrossing their mothers: gospel study, self-improvement, home industry, and compassionate service.

The success of these early Primary groups in reaching their goals for children did not go unheeded or unappreciated by the brethren, who followed their progress closely. One bishop congratulated the Primary children of his ward on their accomplishments, saying that "he felt grateful to see what had been done toward improving the minds and developing the energies of the young." The stake president also commended them and desired them "to become acquainted with the arts and sciences as well as their religion as that would bring this kingdom in advance of all others in all things." He encouraged the officers "to continue in patient labor," and asked "the blessings of God to rest upon all who were interested in the welfare of the children of Zion."[18]

But if Primary meetings reflected the interests of the sisters, they also reflected the fact that children are children and have their own ideas as well. Attendance at meetings was rarely over half the number enrolled, and punctuality was frequently the topic of exhortations. In one Primary a special day was planned as a surprise reward for the children:

> The President...arranged the children by two, and marched them to the new Society House close by, where they were surprised by the sight of buns, tarts, candy and good things neatly arranged upon low tables, to which they were seated; Bishop Price asked the blessing, and while they partook of the feast prepared, showed them the necessity of having their names enrolled, so they could partake of the feast, and narrated the history of the Supper of the Great Bridegroom. We had a large attendance that day, and several came who never attended the meeting before.[19]

Apparently the party had been no surprise; the next week attendance had again fallen off sharply, and the counselor chided those present:

> I notice there is quite a falling away since last Thursday which should not be. [The president] got up that amusement to encourage you to come to these meetings; a great many partook of that feast, that seldom attend the meeting; consequently they did not receive it as a reward, those who attend regular and give attention while there were worthy of what they received.[20]

Women who had decided they could effectively discipline and teach unruly children now faced the reality of managing up to a hundred children ranging in ages from four to fourteen sitting together in one room for at least an hour. In December 1880 members of the Salt Lake City Eighth Ward Relief Society were "exhorted to attend the children's Primary and try and help Sister Fletcher keep the little ones quiet."[21] The same year the Primary president of the Seventeenth Ward decided that maintaining order and interest was too much for the presidency, and "if the mothers could not take an interest in it, she felt it too much of a task, and wished to resign the position." She was released and both of her counselors resigned within a month.[22]

Childish antics as well as maturing accomplishments were both part of the experience shared by children throughout the Church during these early days of Primary. Though local variations were endless, the overall pattern of the program was remarkably uniform throughout the territory. There was no central policy-making board for the Primary during this period. A general Primary president, two counselors, a secretary, and a treasurer were called by the First Presidency of the Church in 1880, but they did not assume a controlling leadership role until well into the 1890s. Instead, the admonitions of respected Relief Society leaders such as Eliza R. Snow were followed, and sisters throughout the Church shared their experiences, responding to general mandates, such as home industry, through an intricate and yet somewhat informal network that existed among the women of the Church.

Almost from the beginning local Primary associations were supervised by strong and viable stake organizations. The first stake board was organized in the Salt Lake Stake June 19, 1880. Ellen Spencer Clawson, the older sister of Aurelia Spencer Rogers, was named the first stake Primary president. A month later the Salt Lake Stake entered an elaborate float in the Church's Jubilee Celebration held July 24, 1880:

> Forty-two children—21 boys and the same number of girls, representing the 21 bishops' wards of this city, all dressed in white, and seated in the sleigh "Julia Dean," which was placed on wheels and beautifully decorated. It was drawn by six white horses, and above on a tall mast was a banner of pure white, with the words, "Primary Associations—Of Such is the Kingdom of Heaven." Over the heads of the little ones was a canopy to shade them from the sun. In front, on

each side of the driver, was a little wood nymph, seated and holding a silken rein, attached to the mouths of the swans' heads on the sleigh, and behind were two little sailors holding the ropes steadying the awning and the banner.[23]

The stake board already had an established forum in the women's conferences held in each stake periodically. They simply added a meeting where problems and projects of the Primary were discussed. The Salt Lake Stake began meeting in such conferences that fall. (The first general Primary conference was not held until nine years later.) Minutes show that leaders from other stakes would often attend the Salt Lake Stake conference and report on the work in their home wards.

Without doubt, the unsung leaders of the Primary during the 1880s were the hundreds of local and stake presidents throughout the territory. Some of these women served in their positions for decades and thus built the strong foundation upon which the general board could build and from which it could draw strength and experience in the coming years. Ellen Clawson in Salt Lake City, Aurelia Rogers in Davis County, Jane Molen in Cache Valley, and Sarah Roberts in Utah Valley are examples of these strong stake leaders who did much of the work during these years.

Jane Molen was called as the first president of the Cache Stake Primaries in 1881 and was not released from this position until 1901, when the stake was divided into three stakes. "After the Cache Stake was organized," she recalled:

> I was chosen and set apart as was the custom in those days, by Eliza R. Snow, as president of the Primary of Cache Stake of Zion, which at this time was from Oxford, Idaho and Malad, Idaho, on the north, to Paradise, Utah on the south. I immediately started to go from one settlement to another organizing the Primaries. I worked alone at first, and then I chose two counselors, Annie Pike and Adeline Barber. There were no board members in those days. I traveled by train, by buggy and by walking, and Saints in the various towns would carry me to my next locations. Sometimes we walked many miles, staying with the Saints.[24]

Jane then described some of her activities during the undoubtedly hot summer of 1884:

> On the 4th of July 1884, Aunt Zina [D. H. Young]
> and Zina Williams visited at my home.... Aunt Zina Young
> spoke of the persecutions of the Saints; many had tears in
> their eyes.... I was busy for the next few months visiting
> Primaries, starting with Paradise, then the meetings in
> Hyrum. I traveled to Wellsville, Mendon, across the valley
> to Providence and Millville.... The next day I visited Primary
> at Paradise. I then went to Mendon to visit Primary and to
> Petersburg [Petersboro] where we organized with Sister
> Ferrell as president. From there Sister Kirby accompanied me
> to Smithfield for a surprise party for Sister S. Barber on her
> fiftieth birthday. We then traveled to Malad City with
> C[harles] O. Card. We decided to go to Hampton, so we
> walked the three miles arriving at Brother Standing's at sun-
> set. We returned and had a meeting at Malad. From there we
> went to Washakie, the Indian reservation. Brother and Sister
> Dredge took us. I was pleased to see the Indians in their own
> Primary meeting. We then traveled to Samaria calling on
> Bishop Stewart's second wife, who had a young baby. I
> named her, calling her Zina after my dear friend who was
> with us, Aunt Zina Young. We returned to Hyrum where
> we both had a rest, as we had been traveling a long distance.
> Here we had a special Primary meeting.[25]

Hours spent in a dusty buggy or walking in the hot summer
sun were typical labors of many of these pioneer workers. The
Indian Primary at Washakie is an excellent example of the varied
fruits of these labors.

One of the features of the Cache Valley Stake Primary, as with
many other Primaries of this period, was the use of a nickel fund
to assist the poor, contribute to the building of temples and meetinghouses, acquire libraries, and help maintain the Deseret Hospital. In a conference of Primary children in June 1884, President
Molen thanked the children for giving enough nickels to enable
four children of a family in England to immigrate to Utah. Now,
she said, the mother was coming to America also because of the

generosity of the children. But there was still a seventeen-year-old boy left to come. Would the children be willing to dig into their pockets a little deeper and find some more nickels so that the boy might be able to come to America with his mother? They evidently responded, because the minutes of the Primary conference a year later report that the mother and her family had all been reunited.[26] One of these children, a boy named James, occasionally drove President Molen's carriage as she traveled throughout the Cache Valley Stake.

Aurelia Spencer Rogers, first president of the Farmington Primary, was later called as the first president of the Davis Stake Primary. Like Jane Molen, she also dedicated hundreds of hours to the Primary as well as to her pressing personal responsibilities. "I smile when I hear modern mothers say they can't find time to teach Primary," she once commented.

> For sixty years I did my big wash by hand; I kneaded and baked bread sometimes twelve loaves a day; sewed all our clothes with a needle and thread and thimble; swept my floors with a broom made from willows I gathered on the river bank; scrubbed my furniture with sand and rags. I've worked in the fields; I've battled grasshoppers; I supported a large family while my husband was on a mission. I did have hardships and sorrows, but it was a good life because I loved my husband, my children, my neighbors and my home. Above all, I loved my Heavenly Father.[27]

Understanding the extent of the additional burden that working in the auxiliaries entailed, Eliza R. Snow closed a letter to Aurelia Rogers in 1881 with the line, "Praying that you and all the dear sisters may have health and strength equal to your arduous labors and noble desires."[28] All of the unnumbered sisters who, like Jane Molen and Aurelia Spencer Rogers, gave countless hours to the Primary were also heirs of that fitting prayer.

On June 19, 1880, a general president for each of the women's auxiliaries was sustained at a women's conference of the Salt Lake Stake held in the Assembly Hall on Temple Square. Eliza R. Snow, who, as mentioned earlier, was officially sustained as general president of the Relief Society, had a hand in selecting all the general officers appointed at the same time. More than a month before the June meeting Sister Snow visited the Twelfth Ward Primary in Salt Lake City, presided over by Ellen Clawson. Aurelia was visiting her sister and recalled talking with Eliza at that meeting:

> ...Sister Eliza, being one of the visitors, came to me and said it was thought best to have some one appointed to preside over all the Primary Associations in the Territory. She suggested that the person should reside in Salt Lake City, as that was the center; and asked me whom I would propose to fill the office.
>
> I said I could not tell on so short notice, but would reflect a few moments. After doing so the name of Sister Louie B. Felt came to my mind. As soon as I told Sister Eliza, she said that was her choice and also Sister Clawson's. This satisfied me that Sister Felt was the one to hold that important office.[29]

Louie B. Felt had been presiding over the Primary Association in the Eleventh Ward, the second group to begin meeting after Farmington and the first to meet in Salt Lake City. She was thirty years old and had been married to her husband, Joseph H. Felt, for fourteen years. Like Eliza, she was childless. She had been working as a counselor in the Salt Lake Stake Young Women's Mutual Improvement Association organized the year before, had conducted a very successful Primary in her own ward, and had taught Sunday School as well. Though she did not have the executive experience of Eliza R. Snow, her pleasing personality was infectious, especially with children. A friend in her ward recalled:

> Sister Felt had wonderful vision and initiative. She seemed to know the soul of a little child, its needs and its possibilities for development, and how to cultivate the best in each. When she called, the children rallied, eager to respond to her persuasive entreaties, her cheerful smiling reproofs. Whether asked to pray aloud or in concert with her, to speak the pieces they had learned, to answer questions, or to keep order, all were willing to try. That was the keynote—anything to win

the approval in word or smile of Sister Felt. Her influence over them was marvelous.[30]

Part of her appeal was that she liked to enter into the games and dance with the children, "a child among the children, happy in the things she and they loved."[31]

Though very much at home in her work with the children, Sister Felt was overwhelmed with a visit from three leading sisters, Eliza R. Snow, Precindia Kimball, and Zina D. H. Young, during the last week in May 1880. She recalled:

[They] said a Central Board of the Primary Association was soon to be organized to look after the interest of the Stake Organizations and they desired to have a President of the Organization. I remarked that I thought Sister Aurelia S. Rogers would be just right. But said Sister Eliza, "It will be necessary to have ones at the head living in the city that we may easily consult with them about the work." ... Then Sister Eliza said, "Sister Felt, we have chosen you for this place." I was so surprised and alarmed that I immediately replied, "I am not worthy and am so ignorant. I could not fill that position. I'm sure I could not." Sister Eliza said, "If you thought you could we would not want you." ... We talked some time about the matter and when the sisters saw how I felt they gathered around me and Sister Eliza gave me a grand blessing.[32]

In June 1880, the conference was held in which the general officers of the Primary and a central board were selected and introduced to the women and children in attendance for their sustaining vote. What an impressive sight this must have been — the entire center section of the Assembly Hall filled with children, each one raising his hand high to sustain the new officers: Louie B. Felt as general superintendent, Matilda M. Barratt and Clara M. Cannon as counselors, Lillie T. Freeze as secretary, and Minnie Felt as treasurer. Eliza R. Snow, who conducted the meeting, then asked the children whom they would like to have speak to them. The children voted overwhelmingly to hear from the prophet, President John Taylor. After thanking the women for their commendable work in behalf of the children, he then spoke directly to the sea of little faces turned upward to hear his words: "Children, you ought to be obedient to your parents and pray morning and night for them and for your presidents, that they may be under the inspiration of the Lord, and God will bless you and give you blessings upon blessings and he will build up Zion...."[33]

Louie Felt had been understandably reluctant to be thrust into the limelight at this historic gathering. Though she had always been popular and one of the leading members of her Salt Lake City ward, she was personally shy and preferred to remain in the background. She was not well acquainted with either the leading sisters or the leading brethren of the Church. Her own father and mother had joined the Church in the 1830s but had remained in their Norwalk, Connecticut, home until immigrating to Utah in 1866. Louie and her husband, Joseph, whom she had met on the trip west, had spent the early years of their marriage in Nevada before settling in Salt Lake City in the 1870s, so most of Louie's life had been spent far from Church headquarters.

Unauthorized to organize Primaries, she found few occasions to visit outlying settlements. Moreover, she seemed to feel more comfortable in her own familiar niche and continued to serve as president of her local Primary association, with few interruptions, until the 1890s. Until the mid-1880s she also continued to visit various Salt Lake Valley wards as counselor to the president of the Salt Lake Stake YWMIA. At the women's conferences of the stake, she was more likely to speak at the meetings of the young women than those of the Primary.

Eliza R. Snow, on the other hand, as the highly lauded president of the Relief Society, was a strong personality and a much-sought-after speaker. In many respects, she acted as *de facto* leader of the Primary, demonstrating her own continuing personal interest in the education of children. Her death in December 1887 was understandably a blow both to the Primary organization and personally to Louie B. Felt, who had relied almost exclusively on her advice. "Louie lost her good support and council," wrote a friend.[34] The imprint of Eliza's almost legendary personality was strongly felt for years after her death.

Eliza's death meant the loss of a talented and dedicated leader, and this alone portended challenges and trials for the young Primary Association, but 1887 marked a challenging time in other ways as well. Louie B. Felt, now alone in her leadership responsibilities, was particularly affected by the difficulties that came at this time to the Church as a whole. The antipolygamy measures, enacted and enforced during the 1880s, brought great hardship to many Mormon families. "We all scattered—for nearly four years," recalled Lillie Freeze, secretary of the Primary general board.[35] Lillie was gone from Salt Lake City for over three years, and Louie Felt left the city twice for extended periods of time. For this reason too, then, Louie's leadership during these years was limited. "Nothing could be done, only as the *stakes* and *wards* kept the work going," recalled Lillie. "And they did *marvelous* work—with the children, with the presence of the leading elderly sisters, their councils and encouragement."[36] On the local level there were also difficulties during these years, but, maintained Lillie, "it [was] marvelous the way the Stake Presidents and local officers kept life in the Primary work, many of them suffering as we had done. The real work of these sisters and the children can best be obtained from the stake and local records. *They are worthy of all honor.*"[37]

Another trial for Louie B. Felt during this difficult decade was her own intermittent illness. With that and the other problems she encountered, as late as 1889, she had yet to assume a major leadership role in the Primary organization. However, her continuing interest and dedication to her own ward Primary, interrupted only by her trips away from Salt Lake City and her visits to various local associations, provided a foundation of experience upon which she was able to build an expanded role for herself and her board during the following decade.

During the 1880s, the success of the Primary Association was due in large part to the determination and shared experience of hundreds of women working in the wards and in the well-organized stakes who took seriously their expanded mothering stewardship—to reach all of the children of Zion. By 1889, in spite of the difficult times and the loss of Eliza, the association was an established, integral part of the Church organization. Through it, women had included children in the building of a literal, earthly kingdom of God. The next decade would see the growth in importance and proliferation of the concerns of the general board.

Primary children, Spanish Fork, Utah

Primary officers and teachers on an outing

Chapter Three

Taking the Helm

In the fall of 1889, after almost a year of illness, Louie B. Felt must have been discouraged. The past four years had been years of upheaval and separation from loved ones. The death of Eliza R. Snow in 1887 had deprived her and the Primary organization of a strong leader and counselor. But she had two sources of consolation: her growing friendship with a young English convert, May Anderson, and the Churchwide Primary workers' conference to be held in Salt Lake City that October—an important first.

Louie's husband, Joseph, had been called out of town on business, and he had asked May Anderson to stay with Louie while he was away. May no doubt had happily accepted, since she had come often to the Felt household during the previous six years, following her arrival in Salt Lake City with her family in 1883. On several occasions she had stayed overnight, since the Felts' home was much closer than her parents' to R. K. Thomas & Co., the dry goods store where she worked as a clerk.

May and Louie had first met on the train that carried the Andersons to Salt Lake City. Louie and Joseph had boarded at Morgan, Utah, to welcome family members returning from the East. May Anderson, then nineteen years old and known as Mary, was completing the last leg of a journey begun earlier that spring in Liverpool harbor on the ship *Nevada*. The Anderson family settled in Salt Lake City, and soon thereafter Mary and her mother visited the charming young Louie B. Felt. Despite the difference in their ages, Louie and Mary became immediate friends. It was Louie who suggested that Mary change her name to May in order to avoid confusion with another close friend of Louie's, Mary Ann Freeze.

At first glance the two women might have seemed vastly disparate in background and temperament. When they met in 1883, Louie was thirty-three and childless, had been a lifelong Church member, and had presided for three years over the fledgling Primary organization. Her magnetic personality attracted many friends wherever she went. May, fourteen years younger than Louie, was the eldest daughter of twelve children in a family very inexperienced in the highly organized Church they had joined a few years earlier in England. Before he converted to Mormonism, her father, Bruce Anderson, had been a temperance lecturer traveling throughout Ireland and England. As a child Mary had recited such pieces as "The Lips That Touch Liquor Shall Never Touch Mine" during her father's public meetings. The Andersons moved often and formed few ties outside their own family. May tended the younger children and did much of the housework, which left little time for reading and school.

With their differences Louie Felt and May Anderson tended to complement each other. The association eventually served to buttress a working relationship that became critically important in determining the future of the Primary organization. Long after Joseph Felt's business trip was completed, May stayed on at the Felt home. The two women lived together for nearly three decades, devoting much of their time to the Primary.

It is not surprising that Louie asked May to take minutes for the first Churchwide meeting of Primary officers in October 1889, even though May was not officially a Primary worker. About twenty-five women representing Cache, Box Elder, Salt Lake, Utah, Juab, Sanpete, Sevier, and St. George stakes gathered for the meeting and heard President Felt tell them that the purpose of the gathering was "to encourage, counsel and advise for the mutual benefit and advancement of the Primary associations."[1] Though the effects of this gathering were modest, it represented the beginning of a central Primary leadership that would strengthen with each succeeding decade.

Far-reaching changes from other sources were imminent. In

the fall of 1890 President Wilford Woodruff issued the Manifesto, halting the practice of plural marriage. This decree opened the way for Utah to acquire statehood six years later, and in turn brought the Latter-day Saint community closer to the mainstream of American life. Mormon children had already been affected by legal changes that brought their educational experiences more into line with those of other children. The passage by the territorial legislature of the Free Public School Act in February 1890 meant that with the establishment of tax-supported public schools, Mormon doctrine could no longer be part of secular education. Church members had originally resisted the change, but responded cooperatively when the decision was inevitable.

Louie Felt voiced the concerns of many at the second Primary conference, held in October 1890. "If there was a time when it was important to attend to the spiritual education of our children," she warned, "it is now when so many of our little ones attend the district schools, where religion is forbidden to be taught." She concluded that it was therefore "necessary to take a more general interest in the welfare of the souls of our little children."[2]

Priesthood leaders responded quickly to the problem but did not turn to the young Primary Association for a solution. Instead, upon the recommendation of the First Presidency of the Church, a separate organization for weekday theological instruction for elementary-age children, known as "Religion Classes," was established in 1890. Since two organizations now had the responsibility of providing weekday religious education for the children, the Religion Classes and the Primary Association were often seen as competing for the attention of the children and the loyalty of women called to participate in both. Such overlap and competition would be explicitly dealt with after the turn of the century through the beginnings of correlation in the Church. But in the beginning, with no such programmed cooperation, the Primary was forced as a matter of survival to reexamine its programs, identify the problems, and define its goals.

One of the major problems the Primary faced was, to use a

37

modern term, "a credibility crisis," i.e., a justification of its existence. Eliza R. Snow had had access to the leading brethren, but now she was dead. Initially Relief Society leaders had organized the Primaries, and priesthood involvement had varied greatly from ward to ward. Not all bishops were as supportive as Bishop Hess had been of Aurelia Rogers's undertaking in Farmington. The lament of one Primary worker in a general meeting in Salt Lake City was shared by many of her sisters: "In many of the wards the Bishops were not interested, and we have tried to use our influence that they might become interested in the Primary work."[3] A Primary leader in another meeting concurred that "the officers felt that generally their labors were not appreciated by the Bishops and Stake authorities."[4] No formal structure had been established to keep the priesthood informed and supportive, so it is understandable that priesthood leaders had not turned to the Primary, but had established separate priesthood-directed Religion Classes.

Part of the problem was simply the low profile of the organization. By 1890 each of the other auxiliaries—the Relief Society, the Sunday School, and both the Young Women's and Young Men's Mutual Improvement Associations—had its own periodical. The Primary petitioned for a journal of its own as early as 1893 but was told to wait. The women thought that they might try to sponsor a regular feature in an existing magazine, such as the *Juvenile Instructor,* but nothing came of this plan either. With the death of Eliza R. Snow, perhaps the strongest cord that bound the three women's organizations together was severed. Each of the auxiliaries became increasingly autonomous during the next decade. Primary programs were no longer necessarily an offshoot of Relief Society programs, yet the Primary had no means of establishing a much-needed identity nor a centrally directed network of communication. Although the Primary general board had expanded in 1893 from its original number of five to thirteen, adding additional members each year, their function other than occasional visits to the wards and stakes had not yet been fully defined.

Other Primary problems had been endemic since the founding.

One Primary counselor told the children "she thought they might try to be orderly for one hour and that these societies were for their especial benefit and they should pay attention."[5] This became an oft-repeated entry in the minutes of most associations, as the local presidencies tried to cope with large numbers of children ranging in age from four to fourteen in a single room for an hour or more. Leaders constantly complained that few boys attended, and one stake leader bluntly related in a general Primary conference during this decade that she "found that the work in some associations appeared to be growing monotonous."[6]

Primary leaders suggested some new books for use during this period, most notably the "Primary Helper" series by William A. Morton, a local author of books for children who was also involved with the Religion Classes. Generally the program continued as it was originally set up. But as the framework in which it had evolved changed, the program became less meaningful, especially to a new generation of children.

If Primary curriculum changed little during these first years, the responsibilities of Primary leaders changed even less. Louie B. Felt presided at the annual Primary conferences in Salt Lake City—meetings similar to the women's conferences held in the various stakes all during the 1880s. Women shared ideas, aired complaints, and received encouragement in their labors. As the Primary grew independent of the Relief Society during the 1890s, Louie increased her visiting to the local wards and stakes. Because of the lack of any central Primary funds, she traveled either at her own expense or at the invitation and sponsorship of a local association. One such expedition, a trip to Springville, led to the call of her dear friend, May Anderson, to be secretary of the general board. As Louie was preparing for the trip, May expressed a desire to go with her. Louie's husband agreed to buy them both tickets, but after leaving, Louie became worried about their accommodations. She knew that she was expected but did not know whether two visitors would inconvenience her hostesses. The solution to the problem was to make May a member of the general board and therefore an official visitor with her. May was reluctant to accept the call but responded, "I would like to think that I would always be with you." Later, May reflected on the words that Brother Donelson, a missionary in England, had spoken to her mother years before: "Sister Anderson, the time will come when the name of this little girl shall be known all over Zion."[7] It was an inauspicious beginning for a career that would span a lifetime.

May's call may have seemed to be an afterthought at this time, but it was certainly an inspired call. Lillie Freeze, Louie's long-time friend and associate, remembered that "with May's efficient help Louie seemed to take new interest."[8] In the early years of their association as Primary workers, they were often traveling companions. Hot, dusty buggy rides were still the common lot of general and local Primary leaders. May later recalled one such trip in Idaho:

> Our stake president was the driver and she knew how to handle horses, so this time we were not so very nervous. We had been going about an hour when we reached a bridge which crossed the Snake River where it was deep and wide, but the bridge had gone and we couldn't drive across. At that time there were few homes or even towns in that section and no such convenience as a telephone.
>
> There was only one thing to do, turn back to the nearest crossroads and find another way to reach and keep our assignment. We finally arrived there, two hours late.
>
> The little meetinghouse built of lumber stood in the blazing sunlight, not a tree in sight to suggest shade. As we came closer we decided that surely we were too late. But, no — around the building were grouped a few big heavy wagons indicating how the congregation had traveled and that they were still there.
>
> When we entered the room it was packed with women and children, the floor was bare, a little table at one end serving for the pulpit; on it was a bunch of wild flowers, somewhat wilted with the heat. A path was made for us to reach the table, but to get there it was necessary to step

carefully, for on quilts spread under and around the tables were babies and little children, most of them asleep.

But one can never forget how we were received. The mothers picked up their babies and all stood and sang for us the song of welcome that had been prepared in our honor.[9]

If Louie and May's partnership aroused a new interest on Louie's part in the round of Primary duties, it must have also inspired a joint commitment to find ways to increase both attention and attendance. In 1892 the Sunday School established a normal training class at Brigham Young Academy, and in 1894 model Sunday Schools were established, conducted by prominent educators. Sister Felt was for years a Sunday School teacher as well as a Primary worker, and perhaps these innovations attracted her attention.

In general, both inside and outside the Church, this period witnessed a mushrooming of interest in the education of children. Camilla S. Cobb, an adopted daughter of Karl G. Maeser, later church commissioner of education, had established the first kindergarten in Utah in 1874. The kindergarten movement gradually gained in popularity among Utah's Jewish and Christian women's groups. Since American kindergartens were generally concerned with the moral culture of young children, churches often sponsored the classes, which were usually held in connection with mothers' classes. In 1895 a number of prominent Mormon women, including Sarah M. Kimball, M. Isabella Horne, Elmina S. Taylor, Zina D. H. Young, Bathsheba W. Smith, and Ellis Shipp, banded together to form the Utah Kindergarten Association. One of the movers behind this organization was Camilla Cobb, who by this time was a counselor in the Salt Lake Stake Primary and hence a friend of Sister Felt and May Anderson. She later became a member of the Primary general board.

Such a milieu seems to have encouraged Louie and May to seek training. In 1894 they enrolled in a course in kindergarten principles taught by Alice Chapin. Miss Chapin, a teacher trained in Boston by Elizabeth Peabody, the founder of the first American kindergarten, opened a model kindergarten and sponsored a mothers' class in addition to the kindergarten course. Her work in Salt Lake City was sponsored by the Free Kindergarten Association, a group composed largely of non-Mormon church women, and the Women's Christian Temperance Union.

The next year Sisters Felt and Anderson inaugurated what they had learned by establishing a private kindergarten in the Eleventh Ward. At the same time, Louie Felt was added to the advisory board of the Mormon Utah Kindergarten Association. By Christmas of 1895 the *Deseret Evening News* reported that thirty-one children between the ages of three and six had provided an interesting program at the Eleventh Ward meetinghouse, "being questioned by Mrs. Felt [and] making their own choice of what should be done." Joseph H. Felt gave a brief description of the kindergarten work and its "remarkable progress."[10]

Both women were involved in kindergarten work during the next several years. They operated their kindergarten together for two years, and May continued the work for another two years on her own. She then went to work in the new Kindergarten Normal School at the University of Utah. In 1897 Mary C. May, a graduate of the Chicago Kindergarten College, was brought to Utah to head the normal school and model kindergarten. For four years May worked as her assistant. Together they "firmly established the kindergarten as a permanent factor in the School of Education of the University of Utah."[11]

While both Louie and May were helping to establish the kindergarten as a permanent part of the Utah school system, they were also bringing some of its education principles to the Primary. A co-worker at the time commented that after they had become involved in kindergarten work their Primary work "began to take on definite and steady growth."[12]

In 1895 Louie was still president of the Eleventh Ward Primary, a position she had held since 1878; May was second counselor. That year they called a number of young women as aides or "assistant secretaries" so that the children in the Primary could be divided by age into three classes and taught in separate rooms. Schools in Utah had begun grading in the 1870s and the Sunday School had followed suit, though the Primary and the Mutual Improvement Associations, with public speaking, singing, and recitations and catechisms as their major emphasis, had never required a graded system. But exposure to a more child-centered curriculum, which emphasized the principle that lessons should be appropriate to a child's mental development, convinced Sisters Felt and Anderson that a graded system would reach more children and perhaps attack the roots of chronic discipline and attendance problems. The experiment in the Eleventh Ward must have been successful, for in that same year, 1895, the Primary general board was encouraging Primaries to grade their associations into three groups. By 1896 a stake worker reported to the board that she "had found the associations in excellent order more particularly in the wards where the associations were graded."[13]

Another experiment shared by many of the Primaries during this period was the organization of mothers' classes. Teaching mothers about children and how they learn was an important goal of the kindergarten movement. The Mormon Utah Kindergarten Association and other local church women had organized classes to educate mothers, as had Miss Chapin in her training program and Miss May at the University of Utah. The Primary also endorsed the idea, encouraging local associations to sponsor their own mothers' classes and to develop their own lessons. More interested mothers, they reasoned, would mean more interested children.

Not all Primary workers had the professional background of Sisters Felt and Anderson, however, and many felt uncomfortable with proposed changes. An officer representing the Panguitch Stake reported in April 1896 that the Primaries there had not been graded "because it was not understood, [and she] desired to get some information on that subject."[14] Another stake worker expressed the general insecurity of the local workers in a plea that "we need a plan or guide to help us in our work so we can all work together in unity."[15] In contrast to the preceding decade, local leaders were looking more and more to the central board to provide a plan to unite them in their labors.

In 1896 the Primary was again advised by the First Presidency to give up any idea of a publication for the present. This was a disappointment because such a publication could have provided a means for disseminating the information that the local associations wanted. That year, however, the general officers presented for the first time at the annual conference of stake officers a suggested outline for Primary work. The next year at the annual meeting they distributed a booklet outlining suggestions for celebrating "Jubilee year" in each ward Primary. In 1897, to commemorate the fiftieth anniversary of the Saints' entry into the Salt Lake Valley, the general board suggested that each ward celebrate the birthday of Brigham Young on June 1, and outlined a program. This shift from a locally planned stake celebration to a centrally orchestrated one paralleled the shifting organizational emphasis during these years. After the turn of the century projects sponsored by the general board would proliferate and its stewardship would continue to enlarge.

An appropriate project undertaken by the general board during the Jubilee year, 1897, was the publishing of Aurelia Spencer Rogers's book *Life Sketches of Orson Spencer and Others, and History of Primary Work*. Since the Primary was in a period of transition, it was appropriate to encourage the sisters to look back at the beginning of the organization. Because of her role in the founding of the Primary, Sister Rogers, by then a general board member, always occupied a privileged and honored position in the hearts of the Primary workers, though she never exercised a controlling leadership position. A special project of hers had been this book, which included her own life sketch and one of her father, Orson Spencer, along with an overview of her part in the beginnings of the Primary. In 1896 she had mentioned to a friend on the general board her desire to see the book published. To honor her, the general board decided to sponsor her book.

Each ward was asked to raise money to help underwrite publication of the book. Officers from the stakes were invited to a surprise meeting on Aurelia's sixty-third birthday in September, held in the 14th Ward Assembly Hall in Salt Lake City. A statement detailing the publishing arrangements was presented to Aurelia. For her, the gesture was fitting tribute. "It seemed to me then that the Lord had opened up the way for the publishing of my book in the most pleasing and satisfactory way possible," she wrote. "How could the Primary Association have better expressed great love for me...?"[16]

Stakes and wards had often collected money and sponsored special projects, but this tribute to Sister Rogers marked the first time the general board had collected funds and coordinated such an effort. By the next year the board suggested that the proceeds from the annual entertainment in each ward be divided into thirds—a third to go to the ward, a third to the stake, and a third to the general board. With such a plan the general board could depend on at least some income to help pay for visiting and to support further projects.

With a firmer financial base, the general board, which by the end of 1899 numbered seventeen, decided to publish a "Book of Instructions" outlining the means by which the associations should be graded. Not only would this book provide much-needed help for local workers, but it also would help the Primary to become more fully understood by the priesthood as well.

With so many new efforts afoot, Sister Felt was able to submit an enthusiastic report to the *Woman's Exponent* as the new century commenced. She expressed appreciation for educators who had introduced the idea of object lessons and the kindergarten, and had helped the Primary leaders perceive a direction for their lessons. "And as the care of children is woman's special charge," she concluded, "the new century will see much advancement" because of the possibilities of the newer education added to "those long inherited qualities."[17] Her remarks were indeed prophetic, for the "newer" education, as she called it, became the major thrust of the Primary Association, and a variety of new experiments were imminent for the women in the ongoing quest to fulfill their "special charge."

For new undertakings, 1902 was a landmark year. The First Presidency had given the Primary permission to print a monthly bulletin, provided the women could keep it out of debt—a major emphasis in the Church at the time. To underscore their own commitment to the new magazine and its potential to the Primary Association, Louie Felt pledged her own house as collateral and May Anderson quit her much-enjoyed work at the University of Utah to work full time for the Primary and the new magazine— supposedly a six-month trial period until things were firmly underway. The first issue of the new *Children's Friend* appeared in January 1902 and contained lessons for three grades as well as instructions for Primary officers. Unlike today's magazine, there were no illustrations and no material for children. Instead, stories and thought questions highlighted lessons dealing with biblical and Church history topics. The mothers' classes were turned over to the Relief Society in 1902, but the *Children's Friend* soon included a "Parents" department that served some of the same functions as the class in informing and motivating parents. From the beginning the women intended that the magazine should also be for the children, and by 1906 the magazine included stories, handiwork, and music for them. The magazine was a financial success from the start, never in the red and often showing a profit. By 1906 more than half of the seven thousand officers were subscribing to it.

To insure the continued solvency of all aspects of general board undertakings, a nickel fund was also begun in 1902. Similar to a fund established by the Sunday School in 1891, the yearly nickels from each child and officer replaced the previous method of forwarding part of the proceeds from annual entertainments to the general board. With a somewhat predictable income, the general board could reimburse board members for their visits to the various stakes and also pay for mushrooming expenses—costly office equipment, such as the first mimeograph machine, purchased in 1899, and full-time office help needed to take care of burgeoning correspondence and the publishing of the *Children's Friend*. Gone were the days when Sisters Felt and Anderson would crawl into bed after each day's work and laboriously respond in longhand to requests from their army of Primary workers.

By 1907 the Primary general board had expanded to twenty-six members plus two honorary members, many with a professional background in education. Increasing numbers reflected expanding responsibilities and functions as the Primary became involved in a variety of projects, all of which served to increase its visibility and credibility with members of the Church as well as members of the community. For example, the board published *The Primary Song Book* in 1905. After years of sifting and selecting songs, under the direction of May Anderson, the Primary made its first attempt to update Eliza R. Snow's hymnbook and tune book, which had been reissued through the 1890s. The Primary board also supported the Salt Lake Woman's League in "betterment work," joining in such crusades as petitions against the sale of liquor. But most significantly, at this time it also undertook a project that, though modest in its beginnings, would eventually become one of the lasting contributions of the Primary Association—its hospital for children.

One day Sisters Felt and Anderson saw a crippled boy trying to negotiate the traffic of a busy street and their hearts went out to him. Sister Anderson struck upon the idea of a hospital. "And thinking always of them it came into her ever-active mind that there were many children who, with proper medical attention, might be saved from being crippled and perhaps from early death," recalled Sister Felt of May's idea. "Thinking this, she suggested endowing a room in our LDS Hospital where such children might be taken care of."[18] In May 1911 the board formally decided to furnish two rooms in the Latter-day Saints Hospital, one for boys, one for girls. A hospital fund to be maintained by voluntary donation mostly from the children was established, adding yet another branch to the Primary's financial undertakings. Since there was no

47

room in the LDS Groves Hospital at the time, the Primary ward had to wait until a new wing was completed in 1913.

Though the women's auxiliaries had become increasingly independent of each other since the death of Eliza R. Snow, the Relief Society, the Young Women's Mutual Improvement Association, and the Primary, very much in the spirit of the nineteenth century, unitedly sponsored one dearly held project. During the nineteenth century most ward Relief Societies had built their own separate Relief Society halls. The buildings, financed by their labors, were the center for women's activities in the Church. But the women wanted a central women's building for all of the auxiliaries. Sarah M. Kimball, a counselor in the general Relief Society presidency, expressed their dream at a Relief Society conference in 1896. She told the sisters that she felt it "a humiliation to be without a place of our own. We had contributed to all public places and at all times. Now we want to have a house and we want land to build it on and it should be in the shadow of the temple."[19]

The Primary board had originally met in Louie Felt's home and then had rented rooms in the Templeton Building, on the southeast corner of Main and South Temple streets, dedicating the rooms to the service of the Lord in 1901. In 1900 they joined with the other women's auxiliaries in the quest for a place of their own, with each group to have equal rights and privileges in the proposed building. May Anderson, in a board meeting, "spoke of the necessity of there being a building belonging to women, first as a matter of history, and second as a place for office and meetings." Louie Felt seconded the need and praised "the privilege of having a building opposite the temple."[20]

In 1901 the First Presidency officially gave its support to the proposed Central Woman's Building and contributed a building site on Main Street, opposite the temple. Each of the women's auxiliaries, including the Primary, began to collect funds for the building. President Lorenzo Snow promised the women that as soon as they had collected twenty thousand dollars, construction would begin. In 1907, after Joseph F. Smith became president of the Church, however, plans for the building were changed to include quarters for the Presiding Bishopric, the Religion Classes, and the Young Men's MIA, as well as the women's organizations. The long dreamed-of woman's building was not to be. In December 1909 the Primary moved into its new offices in the Bishop's Building, as the new edifice was called, the first permanent home for any of the women's auxiliaries.

Many women who had contributed money toward their new building were disappointed at the consolidation. Years later when the call went out to Relief Society women, during the presidency of Belle Spafford, to contribute to the construction of the Relief Society Building in Salt Lake City, an elderly woman from Hurricane, Utah, visited Sister Spafford, climbing the long flight of stairs in the old Bishop's Building because she was afraid of the elevator. She explained that she had brought five dollars to contribute to the new building, but she wanted to know what had happened to the five dollars she had contributed many years before for the construction of the Woman's Building. Somewhat taken aback, Sister Spafford explained that the Relief Society as well as the other women's organizations had been well housed in the Bishop's Building since the time it was erected, rent free. Moreover, she explained, all of the money the Relief Society had raised toward the Woman's Building that had been utilized in the construction of the Bishop's Building was to be returned to the auxiliary for the Relief Society Building. And so, she told the woman, "You have contributed ten dollars to this building." The visitor could only exclaim, "I'm glad to know the Brethren are honorable men."[21]

Despite the initial disappointment, the move reflected a number of changes in the Church at that time. The Primary and the Young Women's MIA were no longer offshoots of the Relief Society. In fact, with a new emphasis on education, the Primary and both the Young Women's and the Young Men's Mutual Improvement Associations were invading a field long dominated by the Sunday School. At the same time a move to revitalize the priesthood quorums tended to multiply the number of priesthood-sponsored activities and to enhance the educational role of the priesthood quorums. This multiplying of programs and over-lapping of concerns created a need for some kind of coordination among organizations and led directly to a series of correlation attempts that would continue over the next half-century. Corre-lation also meant greater priesthood supervision of all of the auxiliaries.

A committee "to adjust the lesson work of organizations so as not to conflict"[22] was established in 1907 with Dr. James E. Talmage as chairman. Hyrum M. Smith and George F. Richards, both members of the Council of the Twelve, were assigned as ad-visers to the Primary two years later. The Primary was the first auxiliary to have advisers; within a few years all of the auxiliaries had them. The women welcomed these developments, because for the first time all of the auxiliaries were being integrated into an overall Church plan. The Primary had been struggling for twenty years to define the goals of its programs, and a concerted common effort on the part of all Church groups to eliminate conflicts and to define areas of responsibility was long overdue.

The specific accomplishments of early priesthood advisers and of this first coordinating committee are difficult to ascertain. At the very least such attempts focused explicit attention on critical needs and sparked some initial attempts to define goals. The actual work of the committee, however, did not directly affect the Primary for some years. That would wait until the organization of the Church Correlation Committee in 1913. By that time the Primary would have defined its goals sufficiently to be in a good position to cooperate with the new committee.

Sister Felt and Sister Anderson as well as other general board members who had been called during these years of vigorous change and growth were committed to the "newer education," as Louie Felt termed the movement that later became popularly known as "progressive education." Many leaders in the other auxiliaries were similarly impressed with the more child-centered education and found many tenets in keeping with larger gospel principles. How to implement these ideas was the critical question, and Primary leaders had been casting about for answers to this question since the 1890s.

National proponents of the movement for child-centered education regularly found their way into the *Children's Friend*. G. Stanley Hall, Francis W. Parker, Marietta Pierce Johnson, and John Dewey were all quoted at one time or another about the need to mold meaningful educational experiences into the lives of children. The new education advocated the importance of loving and dedicated teachers and the necessity for stimulating interest through "doing" exercises, such as singing, dancing, creative play, drama, arts and crafts, and the exploration of nature. It stressed development of both the body and the mind, and the importance of physical and emotional readiness as well as intellectual preparedness in determining a child's level of learning. It also promoted cooperation between the home and the school in creating an environment conducive to learning.[23]

The first lessons printed in the *Children's Friend,* written by May Anderson until 1916, replaced the catechisms and recitations with stories and thought questions. The art of telling stories to capture a child's interest was emphasized repeatedly in conferences and in general board meetings. Sister Anderson told the board members that "there was a great difference between the telling, and reading of a story.... [that] she would change the places in the story and names of the people and bring them nearer home by using local names and places." She then demonstrated her point by telling the story of the ten talents, giving modern names to the persons to whom the talents had been given and developing the idea of "helpfulness" by thought-provoking questions.[24]

At the same time, however, repetition and memorization, anathemas to many progressive educators, were still stressed as important learning exercises. "Have the memory gem learned by the children. Let them say it in concert and also encourage them to say it alone," teachers were counseled in the *Children's Friend.* "Do not be afraid of repetition, we learn things only in that way."[25] Perhaps seeing danger in the overemphasis of such an idea, the *Friend* also included the following advice during these years: "Do not moralize or ask for promises of obedience; do not say that the lesson for today is so and so, but tell stories, sing songs, and recite memory gems."[26] The Primary seemed to adopt a pragmatic mix of traditional methods, such as memorization, with newer techniques, such as open-ended questioning and storytelling.

Although the Primary had committed itself to teach the children the principles of the gospel, the women came to believe more and more that a variety of activities would bolster lagging attendance. Annual statistics still showed that only about fifty percent of the boys and girls enrolled actually attended Primary. In 1905 the board discussed the advisability of giving the older boys some handwork to do, such as making wood models, in order to get them to attend the meetings. Another suggestion was to organize a department of physical culture for both boys and girls. Some board members suggested that nature lessons, ethics, and other such topics be taught along with theology. All of these ideas corresponded with the methods of teaching advocated by the new education, and in 1909, to better facilitate those methods, Primary children were organized into five age groups with two age levels comprising each group.

The board began to investigate these alternatives more thoroughly to discover ways to buoy up the children's interest in Primary. The next year, as a first step in instituting a more child-centered, problem-solving curriculum, it voted to emphasize "ethical subjects and literature." By 1912 the Primary program had expanded to encompass social activity, ethics, and music.

The years between 1890 and 1912, then, were crucial to the Primary organization. Freed from many of the unsettling problems of its first decade, the Primary was able to consolidate its strength and look to the needs of the changing times. Happily for the Primary, these years saw the transformation of the growing friendship between Louie Felt and May Anderson into a productive working partnership in the interest of the Primary. Fortified with new training and skills, these two women, with the help of many other competent and energetic women and the support and advice of enthusiastic priesthood leaders, established the foundation of most of the major projects promoted by the Primary during the next decades—curriculum planning, the magazine, and the hospital. All of these projects would be elaborated upon and expanded, but the crucial philosophical underpinnings and institutional foundations had been laid.

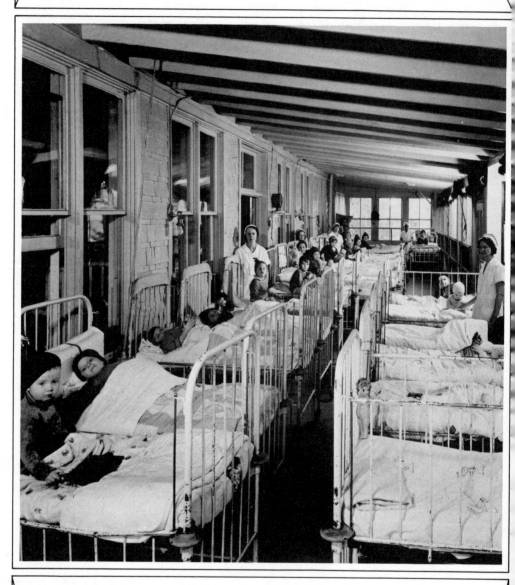

Patients at the original Primary Children's Hospital, Hyde home on North Temple Street, Salt Lake City, Utah

Chapter Four

"For the Betterment of Children"

Over a hundred women crowded into the Primary general board's reception room in the Bishop's Building on June 7, 1913. The general board members had been invited there by a class of nearly 130 women who had just completed a six-week training seminar for Primary workers. "We went, not knowing what to expect," recalled one board member. They were greeted with a shower of flowers and a painting appropriately titled "A Little Child Shall Lead Them." Touched, Louie B. Felt sobbed the thanks of the entire board and then the entire group of sisters "all cried together."[1] The Primary teachers' course of 1913, which thus became history, was a fitting symbol of the growth in organization and scope of the general board.

Members of the board, for the most part women professionally trained as teachers, had been prayerfully considering changes and new directions for their program for a decade. With impetus from the first Churchwide coordinating committee, organized in 1907, the board had finally agreed in 1912 that the Primary curriculum would include social activity, ethics, and music, and had appointed committees to develop such a program. This agreed-upon emphasis reflected the board's commitment to the principle of progressive education, which was child-centered and activity-oriented. In 1913 the Primary introduced a new program representing the most clearly defined attempt so far to incorporate these ideas.

Many of the Primary workers who would be expected to implement this admittedly complicated new program were women with

55

families and many additional responsibilities. Few were trained teachers. "How to place in the hands of our workers the most effective means of promulgating the Church doctrines among the boys and girls of Zion...has been a much mooted question, and one difficult to solve," acknowledged an article in the *Children's Friend.*[2]

As a solution, the general board proposed a six-week Primary teachers' class, originally planned for the fall of 1912 but postponed until the next spring. The board agreed to pay transportation costs of one person per stake. Classes in lesson development, stories and storytelling, music, physical training, domestic science, and hand-work were offered. Each participant was expected to return to her stake and train specialists on the stake board, who would in turn help the sisters in the individual wards. "The idea had its origin in years of experience with the inexperienced," explained the an-nouncement in the *Children's Friend.* Local Primary workers were already "learned in the ways of love and human helpfulness; strong in the desire to serve God," but the Primary teachers' class would help them to become learned in the ways of an experienced teacher as well. [3]

"A pair of bloomers and blouse or middy for gymnasium work are needed," noted the instructions to those attending the class.[4] The physical training class met daily with the stated objec-tive of showing "the purpose of physical training in its broadest sense; also its relationship to Primary work; giving material not only for the children, but for the personal benefit of the teachers."[5] The women not only learned folk dances and games to teach the children, but also studied general health and first aid and worked on systematic personal exercise programs based on individual health assessments and evaluations. Each course was just as meticulously planned, balancing practical hints for teach-ing with background work for the enrichment of the women. Lectures were given by prominent educators and outlines were furnished in each department to provide a concise resume and to assist in taking notes.

The venture was declared an unqualified success. Lillie Freeze, who had been a member of the general board since the 1880s, wrote a poem for the *Children's Friend* comparing the class to the acorn that grows into a "mighty oak." "May the new born class yet prove to be/The root of wondrous primary tree;/Its branches spreading to ev'ry stake,/Where all may of its fruit partake."[6] Twenty-five women from only five of the thirty-two organized stakes had reported at the first general Primary meeting in Salt Lake City in 1889. In contrast, 126 women from nearly all of the northern sixty stakes attended the six-week course in 1913. The final line of Lillie's poem, "See how the primary work has grown," must have been a satisfying thought to Louie Felt and May Anderson, who had attended both the first general conference and the teachers' class and had been instrumental in achieving the growth that marked the two meetings. And the Primary teachers' course of 1913 was only the beginning of many well-planned projects to be executed by Primary workers.

The new curriculum maintained the five age groups that had been prescribed in 1909: Group 1—four- and five-year-olds; Group II—six- and seven-year-olds; Group III—eight- and nine-year-olds; Group IV—ten- and eleven-year-olds; and Group V—twelve- and thirteen-year-olds. All groups met together for opening exercises and then separated for class work.

Under the new program a different kind of activity was stressed each week. A particular theme, such as courage, was developed each month, with a lesson the first week during the Lesson Hour, crafts and handiwork the second week during the Busy Hour, stories the third week during the Story Hour, and games and dances the fourth week during the Social Hour. Thus both the physical and spiritual needs of the child were addressed and, with a minimum of moralizing and lecturing, the curriculum was made more child-oriented.

Children still learned "memory gems" during the Lesson Hour, but the teacher was encouraged not to lecture, and the children did not recite poems, dialogues, and recitations. Instead, the teacher illustrated her point by telling stories and by asking open-ended or thought questions. During the monthly Story Hour the teacher told additional stories to illustrate the month's theme, but had the added responsibility of helping the children develop a taste for good literature and encouraging home reading. One week was devoted to handwork—everything from washing dishes, chopping kindling, making boxes, planting gardens, and helping with spring housecleaning, through preparing picnics, piecing quilts, and making pinwheels, bookcases, and Christmas decorations. The Social Hour generally meant games, such as Fox and Geese chase, the Fairies' Ball, and the Goblin, or dances, such as barn dances, Indian dances, and polkas.

Another experience shared by many Primary children was reading or hearing stories from the *Children's Friend.* By 1913 the magazine featured more material for children, including stories and poems with a few simple black and white illustrations. Many children must have waited for the magazine each month that year to see if the mysterious Princess Wisla would finally discover she was really little Peggy Piper. Little Peggy Piper had lost her memory and almost drowned but was saved by the old Indian Minnie-Lackee, who took her as her granddaughter and tried to hide her identity from the frantic and increasingly desolate Piper family. The story ran for twelve installments during the year along with such stories as "Procrastinating Polly," "Mud's Peculiarity," and "The Little Boy Who Tried to Help" and poems such as "When Godfrey Grows":

> I guess that days we stay the same,
> There's so much else to do
> In school and play, so I must grow
> At night, I think—don't you?⁷

Short verses reminded the children to be good:

> Listen, my boy, I've a word for you,
>   And this is the word: Be true, be true!
> At work, at play, in darkness or light,
>   Be true, be true and stand for the right.

And you, little girl, I've a word for you,
   'Tis the very same: Be true! be true!
For truth is the sun, and falsehood the night,
   Be true, little maid, and stand for the right.[8]

Games to be played at home or at Primary were also included in the magazine. A favorite with the children was the blindfold game, in which one child was blindfolded and a whistle attached to a long string was tied around his neck, dangling down his back. The other children would try to get the whistle and blow into it without being caught.

The new curriculum had been planned during 1912, and the magazine followed by reflecting a new emphasis on social activity and ethics. Such an emphasis was further mandated by the Correlation Committee, which began meeting in January 1913, just as the new curriculum was being introduced. This committee was organized "for the purpose of preventing unnecessary and undesirable duplication of work in the various auxiliary organizations of the Church, and for the further purpose of selecting suitable dates for the holding of stake meetings called by the auxiliary associations and for the general purpose of unifying the work and advancing the cause of each organization."[9] Representatives of the Relief Society, Sunday School, Young Men's MIA, Young Women's MIA, Primary, and Religion Classes served on the committee.

With increasing numbers of stakes and the multiplying programs and concerns of all the auxiliaries, coordinating the annual stake visits by members of the various general boards became more complicated. A joint effort by the auxiliaries was imperative to solve such entanglements. Of more fundamental concern perhaps was minimizing the overlap in lesson topics among the various organizations. A report on both of these matters was submitted by the committee to President Joseph F. Smith and his counselors in June 1913. The field of study for the Primary and Mutual Improvement Associations was defined as "practical religion, ethics, economics, sociology, athletics, amusements and outdoor activities." The Religion Classes, Sunday School, and Aaronic Priesthood quorums, all teaching young people of the same age, were assigned responsibility for teaching "sacred scriptures and Church History."[10]

Beginning in 1913, then, the assigned stewardship of the Primary organization and the educational philosophies and background of many of the general board members meshed perfectly. Providing leisure-time activities remained one of the major responsibilities of the Primary as long as the Religion Classes were in existence. The report of a later correlation committee reaffirming this division of roles explained the importance of Church-directed leisure-time activities. The Church was becoming increasingly urban, and urban youngsters had fewer responsibilities and more time on their hands. Physical inactivity was undesirable, and the Church did not wish to relinquish solely to the schools and commercial establishments its responsibility to provide recreation. Church-sponsored recreational programs could have a "deep religious significance" since they could be designed "to retain and ultimately win back the youth of the Church to a vigorous, enthusiastic allegiance to the Gospel of Jesus Christ."[11]

The Primary programs that evolved during the next twenty years developed within the context of this stewardship. For example, in 1914 the *Children's Friend* reported that "it is one of the pleasant duties of Primary Associations to see that the boys and girls are given, from time to time, periods of enjoyment and play."[12] The article then encouraged each ward to establish an outdoor "play center." A model playground built by a ward in Mesa, Arizona, largely with volunteer labor and materials was enthusiastically recommended: "It has increased the attendance at Primary Association and is helpful in furnishing a place for the little tots during Sunday afternoon church."[13]

In response to its stewardship over recreation and amusement, the Young Men's Mutual Improvement Association adopted the activity-oriented Boy Scout program. Since the national Scouting program included twelve- and thirteen-year-old boys, in 1913 these boys were transferred from the Primary into the MIA to insure the continuity of the program. The Young Women's Mutual Improvement Association did not adopt the parallel Campfire Girls program, but devised a similar group of its own called Beehive Girls. Twelve- and thirteen-year-old girls were not included at that time, however, and remained in the Primary. Most Primary leaders, along with the brethren, felt that it would not be proper to allow such young girls to go out in the evenings and participate in the MIA program, although some wards did allow these younger girls to participate in Beehive Girl activities. Twelve- and thirteen-year-old girls who stayed in Primary were disappointed to remain with the children and not be allowed to attend with the boys their age.

By 1922 Primary board members realized that to solve this problem they needed to build a program similar to that of the Young Women's Beehive Girl program that could hold the interest of these older girls. The Seagull program, spearheaded by counselor May Anderson, was proposed. A small furor over the proposed name resulted when the "Order of the Seagulls," a girls' organization at the LDS High School in Salt Lake City, protested the use of their name by the Primary. The girls even took their complaint to the First Presidency, but the dispute was finally resolved peacefully when a committee from the general board met with the girls, who then agreed to allow the Primary to use the name.

Beginning in 1922, twelve- and thirteen-year-old Seagull girls learned to preside in their own meetings, to take accurate minutes, to give lessons, to tell stories, and to direct play and work. They were given a "student teaching" experience with the younger groups. They made articles for the hospital and held a variety of parties, entertainments, and outdoor activities as well as participated in service projects. A popular aspect of both the Boy Scout program and the Beehive Girls' work in the MIA had been the achievement awards. By completing specific requirements a member could earn special badges and awards. Seagull girls were the first to participate in such achievement programs in the Primary, earning special pins and completing a Seagull scrapbook, which became known as the "Segolia." Symbols, colors, special songs, and costumes were also developed. During the next decade such achievement programs would be devised for many of the younger age groups as well.

Through trial and error the general board was constantly modifying its programs during these years. In addition to the constant thrust to improve the curriculum so it would effectively speak to the needs of the children concerned, the board was also looking for ways to improve the skills of the teachers. A teachers' class similar to the one held in 1913 was cancelled in June 1917 because of the United States' entry into World War I, but the general board constantly included pedagogical methods in the annual Primary general conferences and in stake conventions. The Correlation Committee, which had assigned specific areas of curriculum to each of the auxiliaries in 1913, continued to meet throughout the decade, and by 1917 was addressing itself to teacher training. It was the consensus of the committee that needs would best be served by a central course administered by the Sunday School, which had led out in teacher training. Utah educator Howard R. Driggs was asked to write a manual on pedagogical methods, *The Art of Teaching,* and in 1919 a class based on this manual was offered through the Sunday School of each ward. Teacher training employing a variety of texts was thus centrally administered, first by the Correlation Committee and then by the Church Board of Education. In 1928 the responsibility was returned to the individual auxiliaries.

When the United States entered World War I in 1917, the Primary naturally responded to a call from the Red Cross for help. Since 1880, Primary children had been giving their pennies to support worthwhile projects, and this was but another service they could render. The general board was organized as a unit of the Red Cross to coordinate the "war work"; similar units were organized throughout the Church in the stakes and wards, and by midsummer the children were heavily involved in doing their part for the war effort, which had "need of every Primary officer and child doing everything that [lay] within their power to assist in alleviating the suffering of the millions of men engaged in fighting for their country."[14] By the end of the war the children and officers of the Primary had shipped over 100,000 articles to the Red Cross, including washcloths, comfort pillows, tray covers, hospital bed socks, hot water back covers, comfort kits, bandages, pajamas, and sheets. The children saved fruit stones and nut shells to supply the carbon needed in soldiers' gas masks.[15] And they planted "war gardens," for as the *Children's Friend* counseled: "The Primary Associations can be very useful machines, during the vacation months, in the big task of cultivating and preserving foods against the times of need which appear to be very close to our doors, and perhaps we may be fortunate enough to give some of our plenty to those who are, even now, so much in want of the necessities of life." While they worked, children likely recited such patriotic stanzas as the following, also from the *Children's Friend:*

SOLDIER WORK EXERCISE
(Suitable for Recitation.)
We're First and Second Graders,
    And we snip and snip and snip
To make the little clippings,
    For we all must do our bit.
Hands clean, we don our aprons,
    Then take a little rag
And snip until we have enough
    To fill a one-pound bag.
The clippings then are taken
    And put into a slip
To make a fracture pillow,
    And thus we do our bit.
And we hope, when some poor soldier
    Has been shattered by a shell,
A little pillow we have made
    Will help to make him well.

We constitute the Third Grade,
   And we've learned to crochet
The edges round the washrags
   And we do our bit this way.
If we were only old enough
   We'd go across the sea
And help preserve our country
   As the land of liberty.
....

But what's the use—we're far too young,
   So here at home we'll sit
And quickly ply our crochet hooks,
   For each must do his bit.

We are the high class workers,
   We sew, crochet or knit.
We keep our fingers busy
   For we want to do our bit.
We've learned how our good pioneers
   Who, though so very poor,
Ne'er turned a hungry white man
   Or Indian from their door.
Then we, who are so richly blest,
   Should work and save and give
To help our fellow creatures
   That they may also live.
So let us all keep doing,
   And never idle sit,
For 'tis by work and sacrifice
   That we can do our bit.
                          Edna May Irvine.[16]

Another aspect of the war work that the Primary supported
in the pages of the *Children's Friend* was Children's Year, sponsored
by the Children's Bureau of the United States Department of Labor
and the Child Welfare Department of the Woman's Committee
of the Council of National Defense. During the war May Anderson served on the Utah Child Welfare Committee, which promoted

Children's Year in Utah. "Other warring countries have learned that national security requires the protection of children," explained the *Children's Friend* in announcing Children's Year April 6, 1918, through April 6, 1919. Special attention was to be directed toward five concerns regarding children: public protection of mothers, infants, and young children; home care and income; child labor and education; recreation; and children in need of special care.[17] The *Children's Friend* counseled willing help on the part of Primary workers in following through on one of the first tasks: the weighing and measuring of every child under five years of age by local committees of the Council of National Defense. During this year the magazine also carried a wide range of articles regarding nutrition, hygiene, education, and recreation of children.

Before Children's Year was half over, the war itself was at an end. Because of the influenza epidemic that followed, many Church activities, including Primary, were suspended for a time during the winter of 1918-1919. Sister Felt counseled the workers through the magazine to continue to teach the gospel in the home. But this winter interlude of suspended activity was short, and the range of concerns that the Primary and the other Church auxiliaries resumed had extended far beyond the confines of the home circle.

Joining with other auxiliaries as well as a variety of civic and state organizations, the Primary asked the children to contribute to the Armenian and Syrian Relief Fund and the European Relief Fund. Accustomed to giving, the children contributed over forty-two hundred dollars through their nickel fund to help in Europe and the Middle East, where starvation and disease were left in the wake of the devastating conflict. Relieving the suffering was an important part of the task at hand, but there was a growing feeling within both the Church and the nation that much more could be accomplished with the kind of cooperation that had been engendered by the response to World War I. Such cooperative efforts should be turned to alleviating many of the problems among the populace back home.

In the early months of 1917 before the United States entered the war, the First Presidency—Joseph F. Smith, Anthon H. Lund, and Charles W. Penrose—addressed a joint letter to the general boards of the Relief Society, Young Women's MIA, and Primary Association, stating that "there exists a pressing need of improvement and reform among our young people, specifically in the matter of dress and in their social customs and practices." Warned that "some of the daughters of Zion appear to vie with one another in exhibitions of immodesty and of actual indecency in their attire" and that "both sexes are fast approaching a state of depravity in dancing, and in their feverish pursuit of frivolous and dissipating pleasures," the women were advised to work as a "co-operative unit" to attack the problem. The resulting "Social Advisory Committee," composed of three members from each of the women's general boards with Elder Stephen L Richards as chairman, promptly solicited each woman's loyalty to the challenge: "Officers first, and then members should show by example and precept that they gladly join hands with the Authorities of the Church in the endeavor to overcome the evils which exist."[18] The Sunday School, Young Men's MIA, and Religion Classes soon joined the committee, and within weeks issued a small pocket pamphlet, "Instructions on Social Work," composed chiefly of suggestions on dances and dancing, and another booklet on the subject of appropriate dress. These activities were interrupted by the war.

After the end of the war many members of the Social Advisory Committee felt that the committee's definition of social work should be expanded to include the kinds of concerns faced during the war that especially affected children. Elder Richards returned from a national convention of social workers held in May 1918 and told his co-workers that the discussions at the sessions of the convention opened up in his mind "a field of greater endeavor." He said that the "people of the world are hungry for a system that will lead toward a great central movement for moral uplift, but they have not the units to work through."[19] Certainly the Church had a great advantage in this regard.

In the ensuing months members of the committee considered taking up "some of the problems discussed by professional social workers."[20] They undertook a survey of social conditions, resulting in reports on recreation, health, charities, delinquency, public agencies and institutions, and child welfare—the Primary's contribution. Elder Richards expressed the consensus of the committee: "Many opportunities will be found. Our work will be the most scientific and efficient of any work done, for the spirit of the Gospel will enlighten the true scientist and assist him in devising the most humane methods."[21]

Cooperating fully with the decision of this coordinating committee, the Primary sponsored May Anderson as a delegate to the National Conference of Social Workers held in New Orleans during the spring of 1920. Later, when the Social Advisory Committee assigned social functions to the auxiliaries, the Primary was assigned private care of dependent orphans and neglected children, preadolescent recreation, day nurseries, and training for community service. After conducting a survey of conditions in Salt Lake City, the board decided to accept responsibility for providing a day nursery. In fall 1920 they sent a board member to Denver to take a special twelve-week course in social welfare work and then arranged to have her and others actively engaged in child welfare lecture to them on the subject. The board also ordered textbooks dealing with various aspects of the newly developing social science. With this impetus the Primary actively supported a variety of private and civic ventures concerned with children, such as free kindergartens in neighborhood homes and the Salt Lake Civic Center. Board members lobbied for proposed legislation affecting children, establishing a legislative committee in 1923 to oversee such efforts.

Work on a day nursery and convalescent home for children occupied much of the energies of the board members in the months that followed. They were encouraged, however, by the fact that President Heber J. Grant seemed favorably impressed with their proposals. Since the opening of a Primary-sponsored ward for children in the LDS Groves Hospital in 1913, many Primary workers had cherished the goal of an entire children's hospital; now that dream, planned in conjunction with the newly assigned responsibility for a day nursery, seemed at last a reality. In the summer of 1921 Louie Felt and May Anderson traveled east for the purpose of obtaining suggestions and information from well-established institutions. With the support of local physicians, and with the Presiding Bishopric's assurance that the Church would stand the expense of getting a house ready for use as a convalescent home and day nursery, plans began in earnest during the fall.

As the time for the opening of the new hospital drew near, the general board began to consider seriously what the additional commitment would mean. In February 1922 five children were being treated in the Primary ward at the LDS Hospital, the average expense for each patient being one hundred to five hundred dollars per month. Generally only needy children were admitted, so the Primary was responsible for all expenses. In the new children's hospital at least five times that number could be treated monthly. How to raise additional funds to defray such heavy expenses was a subject of much concern. There was a variety of suggestions: Primary children could raise and sell beans, clubs interested in child welfare work could be asked for donations, advertising through the newspaper could be increased. The suggestion of board member Nelle Talmage was finally adopted: The Primary Associations would hold a "Penny Day" and invite every person in the Church to contribute pennies equaling his or her age. Until 1973 when the Church relinquished control of its hospitals, birthday pennies were a major source of financing Primary-sponsored patients at the hospital.

The convalescent home, originally called the Latter-day Saints Children's Home and Day Nursery and later named the LDS Children's Convalescent Hospital (Louie B. Felt had declined to have the converted hospital named in her honor), was formally opened May 11, 1922, in the refurbished Hyde home on North

Temple Street in Salt Lake City, across from the temple. The day after the opening, an event attended by many Church and civil authorities with President Heber J. Grant giving the dedicatory prayer, two little boys dressed in overalls came to the door and asked if they might come in. "Where's your piano?" one of them asked. "You had one yesterday." The piano had been hired for the opening, it was explained, but the sisters certainly hoped to have another one soon. "Well, then," said the boy, proffering some sheets, "here's some music for you to play to the little sick kids."[22]

The 5,907 "little sick kids" who were cared for by the Convalescent Hospital came to love their temporary home. "Everything we do here is fun," reported one child. "I am so glad for this hospital. I want to thank all the people for giving their pennies so we can come here and be helped." Another patient found the home to be "just like a little town. We have picture shows, doctors, a dentist, nurses, parties, Sunday School, Primary, school, and handcrafts." One child knew firsthand the value of contributing his pennies to the hospital. "I gave my pennies on my birthday to the Primary," he said, "and I am glad all the children give theirs so I can come here and get well with the other children."[23]

The Primary relied on this spirit of giving to furnish many of the articles needed for maintaining the hospital and the day nursery. A Young Mothers Club presented thirteen aprons and three night dresses for use in the nursery with the accompanying note: "We do hope you will find the little garments useful and practical as we—a group of young mothers in the Church—have found real pleasure in making and presenting same to you for such a noble cause."[24] Articles received at the hospital during one year included quilts, nightgowns, sheets, clothing, canned fruit, chickens, turkeys, ducks, eggs, candy, ice cream, potatoes, dried fruit, honey, lard, apples, popcorn, scissors, dolls, books, flower vases, a flagpole, and a canary. The canary, according to the reports of the children, sang with the music during Sunday School but was perfectly quiet during the sacrament service.[25]

In addition to contributing their birthday pennies and various other supplies, Primary children were kept involved with their hospital by letters from the children in the hospital and stories about their recoveries published regularly in the *Children's Friend.* The parents of a little boy who had never walked before coming to the hospital expressed their gratitude to the Primary:

> I want to write to you and tell you how thankful we are to have our son home with us. We have taken the cast off his leg, and his leg seems to be perfect. He walks now without crutches and he can also bend his knee. Dear ones, we have no word to express our thankfulness to you and this wonderful hospital for the care you have given our little son. He is always talking about the Children's Hospital and how he likes it there and how he was treated; he often says he wants to come back and see you all again.[26]

Children were admitted regardless of race, religion, or ability to pay and received the personal care of such women as Anna Rosenkilde, who was appointed superintendent of the hospital. Operations were not performed at the hospital in the early years; it was a convalescent hospital, a place where sick children could recover in a personal, loving, and homelike environment.

An article prepared by the general board for the Red Cross organization in the closing months of 1921 provides a telling self-analysis of the widespread concerns and emphases of the Primary Association that had evolved during the preceding decade of ever-expanding commitments.

> An association perfected for the purpose of assisting in the spiritual, ethical, economical, and physical betterment of children. Organized primarily for benefit and instruction of children of the Latter-day Saints, but membership and betterment work not limited to creed. Fosters state and community child welfare movements. Supports and helps to promote legislative movements to secure enactment and enforcement of proper educational and health laws. Has an enrollment of 60,700 children between ages of four and fourteen years and 10,117 officers. The work is planned and directed by a General Board of twenty-four members. All officers with

exception of four members of General Board, who devote entire time to work, give their services gratis. Weekly meetings are held where, following a definite course of study, children receive moral and religious instruction by lesson and moral story, also are taught to express ideals by means of handwork, dramatization, games and folk dances. The handwork, in addition to teaching moral lessons and encouraging creative genius, develops economy and thrift. Thousands of articles, made largely from old materials, are sold annually in fairs and bazaars. Proceeds of sales are used for running expenses of different branches and surplus used for charity and hospital expenses. During the recent world war the regular classes of this association made and donated approximately 120,000 articles to the National Red Cross. Maintains a child's ward in the Doctor Groves L.D.S. Hospital at Salt Lake City where needy children receive treatment gratis regardless of creed. A large Convalescent Home and Day Nursery is being completed in Salt Lake City. Surveys are being made in Salt Lake City and other localities to search out the needy and to make a systematic study of child conditions and needs in general. Association seeks the further establishment of more and better playground facilities and to provide opportunities for all kinds of directed play and recreation for children. Is active in and gives financial support to Social Welfare League of Salt Lake City, also free clinic and free milk stations. A child's magazine, "The Children's Friend," is published monthly, subscription price $1.25 per annum. A membership fee of ten cents per annum defrays general running expenses and free will contributions help to carry on hospital work.[27]

It is evident that by 1921 the Primary Association was no longer seeking an identity!

In the fall of 1925, after forty-five years as general president of the Primary Association, Louie B. Felt requested that she be released from her position. As a leader she had successfully inspired loyalty and arbitrated difficulties. Her personal and spiritual presence had been central to the Primary organization during her

71

many years as president. She once characteristically remarked that "she felt very humble in the part she had been able to play in the Primary work and would like to remain in the background."[28] Organizationally she had remained in the background, willing to defer to Eliza R. Snow during the early years, and later to rely on the support of her counselors, Matilda M. Barratt, Lillie T. Freeze, May Anderson, Clare C. M. Cannon, Josephine R. West, and Clara W. Beebe, who served at various times during her forty-five-year presidency.

Sister Felt's warm manner and her acknowledged spiritual gifts endeared her to associates. She would often bless board members before they visited the wards and stakes. Prayer meetings for board members in distress were held. On one occasion, while visiting a stake with Sister Anderson, she received a note during the meeting asking her to call at a particular home. There she found a gravely ill baby and, at the mother's request, knelt and prayed for the child, promising recovery. As she traveled home she was disturbed at her promise for she feared the child would die. Several months later she received a letter of gratitude from the mother enclosed with a picture of a healthy child.[29]

Unlike her friend Louie, May Anderson, who became the second general president in 1925, was a forthright, candid, and practical woman. "We are always so pleased to get a letter or card from you even though we are so slow in responding. But but! the same old story, too much to do, and the doers in a constant state of being too tired," wrote May to a friend in 1917. The next paragraph of the friendly letter reveals May's characteristic flair for the straightforward comment: "Your flowers came too late for the conference and too wilted to do anything with, but we did appreciate the loving thoughtfulness that prepared and sent them."[30] Her rhetoric is delineated all the more graphically when compared with Louie's glowing greetings in a letter written to the same friend the day before: "Your card, letter, pictures and kind wishes all here before me. And I can't tell you how pleased I was to receive them. I had many letters, telegrams, and various other things on my birthday, but none so dear to me as yours.... God bless and keep you, sweetheart, and return you in safety when you are ready to return to us once more."[31]

Another example of their genuine differences in temperament and manner of communicating occurred when a young girl working in the Primary office was offered an increase of salary from sixty dollars to eighty-five dollars a month if she would join a city firm. Sister Felt's immediate response, undoubtedly influenced by her own sense of loyalty and kindness, was to encourage the young woman to stay with the Primary by offering her a raise of ten dollars per month—a raise that nevertheless fell short of that offered by the other firm. Sister Anderson, with characteristic pragmatism, stated "she did not approve of holding a girl back when she had opportunity to advance and recommended that [she] be permitted to take the new position." She was sure another equally capable girl "could be procured for fifty or sixty dollars." The majority of the board responded to Louie's more empathetic recommendation and voted to keep the young woman with them.[32]

Sister Anderson helped Sister Felt by overseeing many of the administrative decisions and organization details; she in large measure spearheaded the magazine, involvement with the Correlation and Social Advisory committees, curriculum writing, and the building of the hospital. The personal friendship of the two women buttressed this working relationship—a symbiotic partnership in which each compensated for the weaknesses and complemented the strengths of the other. By 1925 the fruits of this remarkable association, supported by the dedicated efforts of hundreds of other women, were unmistakable.

As Sister Felt left the Primary Association, her "child" had definitely come of age. She had nurtured it in its infancy and seen it grow into a self-sustaining organization to bless the lives of children. For a woman who had no children of her own, it had provided her with many children whose spiritual well-being was placed in her hands. As one co-worker wrote of her, "No woman... filled her position better and no one is entitled to more honor."[33]

Margaret Boyle (Adamson), queen of the Primary Jubilee, 1928

Chapter Five

The Primary
Comes of Age

More than ten thousand children from nearly every stake of Zion marched through the streets of Salt Lake City Saturday afternoon, June 9, 1928. The parade, celebrating the Primary's Jubilee (fifty-year) birthday, included floats from nearly all of the one hundred stakes of the Church as well as some of the missions. That evening the throng of children participated in a pageant at the University of Utah stadium depicting the history of the Primary Association. A queen of the Primary with fifty attendants was crowned, and dances depicted the birth of the Primary and early activities, such as making rugs, raising beans and barley, and holding fairs. Current Primary programs were also celebrated in dance and song.

On Friday and Sunday, special meetings were held in the Tabernacle on Temple Square, which was festooned with thousands of paper flowers made by children throughout the Church. "It makes me feel thrilled to know that I am making a flower for the Jubilee to be used in the big Tabernacle," one little girl remarked to her teacher, and thousands of other children must have been similarly impressed with the festivities.

Certainly the great occasion left vivid memories for the Jubilee queen, Margaret Boyle (now Adamson), a Primary girl just seven years old. The elaborate costume she wore while riding on the lovely queen's float, prepared by the Ensign Stake Primary, was beautiful to look at but very uncomfortable to wear. Margaret remembers the numerous fittings in the "cold and slippery lavender satin dress with the rhinestones touching my skin as I pulled it over my curls." The long, regal robe of red and gold with ermine-like trim was fun to wear, but the crown cut into her head until "some dear soul at the costumer's lined the headband with cotton." Who cared if it showed a little bit! Margaret sat enthroned in the heart of a sego lily blossom, attended by fifty brightly costumed children, leading the parade of eighty-five floats and numerous decorated cars. Virtually every Primary child in the Salt Lake City area and many from beyond participated in the celebration, which left lifelong memories for them all.

The Jubilee was first of all a tribute to the hundreds of women who had served in the Primary during its first fifty years. President May Anderson, who celebrated her sixty-fourth birthday during that weekend, had herself worked in the Primary for nearly forty years and therefore fittingly gave the tribute: "To the woman of pioneer days who walked miles because there was no transportation facilities; who did not falter because she needed to be janitor as well as teacher; who carried her fuel after grubbing or chopping it; who cleaned with her own hands that the children might learn that cleanliness is a virtue; who taught without training—trusting in God and His divine words to give the necessary inspiration."[1]

Present and honored were other women who, like Sister Anderson, had grown old as Primary workers—Lillie T. Freeze, a member of the first general board called in 1880; Louise Morris White, one of Louie B. Felt's counselors in the Eleventh Ward in 1878; Jane Molen, first stake Primary president in Cache Valley; and other long-time board members, such as Lula Greene Richards, first editor of the *Woman's Exponent*.

Louie B. Felt, who had served for forty-five years as general president of the Primary Association and had died only four months before the celebration, was eulogized by Lillie Freeze, who recalled that she and Sister Felt had been intimate friends for seven years before the Primary was even thought of. Women such as Louie

Felt had literally given their lives to the Primary, she reminded them. "The pioneers of this work had no precedents to follow; they worked by faith and by obedience to those placed over them. ... These two things carried them through, because no one in that day had the vision to see the development of the Primary Association to what we see it this glorious day."[2]

The Jubilee was also a time for looking forward. Elder Orson F. Whitney of the Council of the Twelve described the changing challenges in his timely address. "You will not have the same tasks nor the same trials as the brave men and noble women who founded this desert-born commonwealth," he told those present. "Your work will differ from theirs as the walls of a building differ from the foundation stones." Continuing with the image, he described the finished walls of the building, contrasting them with the roughness of the foundation stone. "But when men build the walls of a house...they polish and gild, and make the building beautiful, because it is to be seen, and is expected to attract attention, to elicit admiration and praise."[3]

The Jubilee celebration must have been especially meaningful for President May Anderson. She had helped lay the strong, rough foundation stones, but she had also begun the work of erecting the finished walls. In the next decade she would continue to finish the edifice and begin to build a protective fence around it—defending it against change, though some change was inevitable and much of it was beneficial.

May Anderson had been called by the First Presidency to succeed Louie B. Felt as general Primary president on October 6, 1925. Serving with her during her fourteen years as president were three counselors—Sadie Grant Pack and Isabelle S. Ross, who were sustained with her in 1925, and Edna H. Thomas, who joined the presidency at the release of Sadie Pack in 1929. One of Sister Anderson's first projects as president was preparing for the Jubilee celebration in Salt Lake City. Utah was still the center of any such celebration for the Church, but this emphasis was subtly beginning to shift. Gathering to Zion was no longer the message preached to converts. Members were encouraged to stay in their homelands and build up the Church there. Though by the 1920s Primaries were still virtually unknown in most missions of the Church, some Primaries had been established away from the Utah center of the Church as early as the 1880s in Hawaii and New Zealand, but success in those areas had been sporadic and problems constant.

A Primary of thirty-nine children had been organized in Hawaii in 1883 by a missionary and his wife. They reported that the problems of "trying to teach children without having sufficient knowledge of the language to explain things in clearness" along with the lack of "cards and books...to assist in making our meetings interesting to the children" made the work very difficult.[4] Many such early Primaries were short-lived, lasting only as long as a particular missionary remained in the area.

Some of the earliest Primaries in England, established nearly forty years later, were similarly dependent on dynamic missionaries. In December 1919 the Primary in the Handsworth Branch of the Birmingham Conference was the only one operating in the entire European Mission. The first Primary in Europe had been organized in the Hyde Branch in 1916 by the Relief Society president, Florence Allsop, but it did not last long. The Handsworth Branch Primary was organized by Caroline J. Hatch, who was serving a mission in England with her husband, Charles W. Hatch. The branch discovered that some of the poorer children would come to Primary who would stay away from Sunday School because of their worn clothes, but the real success of the venture was definitely linked to the personality of Sister Hatch. While she and her husband remained on their mission, the Primary flourished. With her help the children put on elaborate pageants depicting such events as the Pilgrims' journey to America and the birth and growth of Mormonism. "The Pioneers in fitting array, and the 'Red Men' with their war whoops first brought tears and later laughter to the eyes of the audience," recalled a spectator at one extravaganza. "In fact the pageant was presented in such a way that many investigators present were led to see the overruling power of God in preparing a choice land and guiding a chosen people for the establishment of His Church."[5] The Handsworth Primary tried to follow the lessons outlined in the *Children's Friend,* but with only a few children and a shortage of adult leadership, such an approach was difficult.

Primaries were never successful in the missions until the 1920s, when home and neighborhood Primaries were introduced. One of the first home Primaries, though admittedly an accidental one, was started by Hettie H. Harper in Dudley Port, England. Hettie's mother had died, and she felt responsible to teach her younger sisters the gospel since the family lived quite a distance from the nearest branch. She started holding meetings in her kitchen with her sisters, and in time a few of their friends joined them. "I soon found many others asking for permission to attend our meetings," recalled Hettie.

> After consideration, I permitted all to come who desired. The result was marvelous; children came in great numbers, and we felt that it was brought about through the workings of the Spirit of the Lord.
>
> Then came the problem of making room for them. I seated some on the wooden sofa, some on the table, a few on the sewing machine, one on each side of the fender and the others on the floor. On one occasion the table gave way, but there were no injuries. And there in the flicker of the candle light we learned the Songs of Zion and the teachings of the Lord.
>
> At times I was reminded of the old woman who lived in a shoe; I had so many children I hardly knew what to do with them. They came for the Gospel like the children went after the Pied Piper of Hamlin; there were fat ones and thin ones, tall ones and short ones—they came in droves.[6]

The children were sometimes difficult to handle. Mostly waifs from the street, they were often rowdy, remembered Hettie, "even to damaging the house." She finally asked the missionaries to assist her. "It is difficult for some people to teach children," she admitted of her experience with the elders, and sometimes "the children pray for the stories to be more interesting so that they may understand." Progress was made, however, and Hettie could report:

I have almost forgotten the hard times I used to have, and I am fast receiving the fruits of my labors. The children bring me flowers and many little tokens of love. I dearly love them and would do anything to give them happiness, of which they receive little in their homes. Their leisure time is very limited, and many have to care for babies during the meetings, while their mothers are in public-houses, and elsewhere.[7]

Dudley Port soon had a branch, built around the nucleus of the Primary. Within five years Hettie could proudly exclaim, "Do you know our branch is now fully organized?" There were nearly thirty baptized members, many of them from Hettie's group and their parents. The branch boasted an organ and conducted sacrament meetings, Primary, Sunday School, a genealogy class, Relief Society, and MIA.[8]

In 1922 the Correlation-Social Advisory Committee was discontinued and replaced by the Auxiliary Executive Committee. In April 1924 all of the auxiliaries, including the Primary, submitted proposals to mission presidents gathered for general conference on how they intended to expand their programs into the missions. The idea of home and neighborhood programs was presented there, not without some opposition. "Scattered conditions and lack of workers make the introduction of Primary Association work...impossible at the present time," remarked one president. He said that it was difficult enough to carry on existing organizations, such as the Sunday School, and thought it better to utilize these associations than to attempt to make new organizations.[9]

Primary general board members felt, however, that their new concept would overcome the difficulties mentioned and would reach children who could not attend on Sunday. Moreover, the

Primary could be used by the missionaries to attract investigators. "As a rule, geographical conditions in missions render the holding of Primary Association meetings as such impracticable," the board members conceded in their presentation. But home Primaries could be established with only one Latter-day Saint child, and non-Mormons would make up the majority of such groups. The mission presidents finally agreed to the proposal: "It is not an easy task but we will do all we can."[10]

A concerted effort was made, at the request of Elder John A. Widtsoe, president of the European Mission, to organize Primaries throughout Europe in 1930. Nettie Woodbury Miller was called as a special missionary from Utah to assist. The November 27, 1930, issue of the *Millennial Star,* a Church magazine published in England, was devoted to the Primary. "Dear childless wives or heart-hungry, would-be mothers, or mothers with a little more room in your mother heart," began the editorial, "here is your work and your great calling: To mother some, a few, or even one love-hungry child of the countless number with whom you are all surrounded.... Invite the children from the highways and the byways; all are God's children."[11]

In spite of cooperative effort, the work was always difficult. The *Children's Friend* began to print special mission lessons in 1930, but each mission was responsible for translating the material it felt was applicable. The programs were American in nature; they did not take into account the unique cultural differences in the various countries. Language barriers and competing youth groups offered additional problems.

The Primary supervisor in Norway, reporting in 1938, could not help sounding discouraged, and her report was not atypical: "It is hard for me to give a talk on Primary work for it is the hardest organization we have to carry on successfully." Then she enumerated what the problems were. Children attended school six days a week, leaving little time for outside activities. Inadequate transportation to cover long distances and lack of facilities in which to hold meetings also inhibited the work. In the winter, darkness came early and parents did not want their children out, and in the summer, most children spent their vacations in the country. In addition, there were many organizations for children in that country that furnished all materials without any cost. She noted that where Primaries were successful, it was discovered that the missionaries brought "all-day suckers each week, and when the Elders stopped doing this, the children quit coming." Yet with all the difficulties, she concluded her report with hope: "I feel more encouraged," she said, "than I did last year."[12] The wide-spread employment of women and the attendance of rowdy street children, similar to those with whom Hettie Harper contended in England, added to the problems of making Primary succeed in foreign countries. These problems, in varying intensity, persist in some areas today.

Despite such difficulties, however, dedicated women through-out the missions continued to struggle to build the Primary. "Primary activities seem to be one of the best means of getting into the homes of the parent," remarked a worker in France. "Most parents appreciate the interest shown in their children...."[13] Another leader from Sweden maintained that despite the problems, "the general attitude of the Primary workers is enthusiastic and hopeful."[14]

As faithful leaders in the various missions strove to make the Primary programs work, the general board continued to modify and experiment with the curriculum in Primaries throughout the established stakes of the Church. The Seagull program, introduced in 1922, had been highly successful in motivating twelve- and thirteen-year-old girls to stay in Primary. The women now began to discuss what they could do to increase enthusiasm for Primary among the next older group of children—the ten- and eleven-year-olds. The boys were of particular concern. More girls than boys had always attended Primary; many boys seemed to feel that it was sissy and, if they came at all, were prone to skip off early. Some of the board members began to agree with the boys, and committees were appointed to brainstorm ideas for ten- and eleven-year-olds. The board struggled to devise "some scheme whereby children might be given credit for work accomplished."[15]

In 1925 Primary leaders introduced the Trail Building program. Ten- and eleven-year-old Primary boys were christened Trail Builders, "because of the boy's natural tendency to trail out." Boys earned felt emblems to be sewn on a bandelo for specified tasks completed. A green felt hat with a picture of a pine tree completed their uniform. A special cheer, B-T-B-O-T, meaning "Boy Trail Builders on Top," was designated for times when boys needed a "spontaneous jubilant expression." The program also included a hymn, a code, a special alphabet, a salute, and a motto for appropriate occasions. The girls of the same age were called Bluebirds. Blue beads strung into a necklace or bracelet and scrapbooks chronicled their achievements. A headband decorated with bluebirds and a bluebird pin completed their regalia.

In 1928 the next younger group, composed of eight- and nine-year-olds, was given a name as well as symbols, colors, mottoes, and scrapbooks. They became Zion's Boys and Girls—the Zeebees and the Zeegees. Zion, they were reminded, stands for "the pure in heart," and they were armed with their symbol, a red and white shield, to remind them that "courage to do right and to live purely is my shield against sin and failure." The twelve- and thirteen-year-old girls were still Seagulls, the four- and five-year-olds remained in Group One, and the six- and seven-year-olds comprised Group Two.

When the Religion Classes, which had long held the responsibility for weekday religious instruction for children, were discontinued in 1929, the Primary was asked to assume responsibility for the children's spiritual as well as ethical and physical education. At the same time a suggestion was made to transfer the twelve- and thirteen-year-old girls into the YWMIA. The boys of that same age group had been transferred to the YMMIA in 1913 in order to take part in the activities of the MIA, receiving their spiritual training in the Religion Classes and later the junior seminaries. But Primary leaders strongly urged the retention of these girls in the Primary. In 1931 the First Presidency suggested that "it would be inadvisable to make an arbitrary ruling to the effect that all girls of twelve and thirteen years of age should attend the Primary Association or to the effect that they should all be enrolled in the Mutuals." But they later agreed that every effort should be made to keep the girls in Primary until age fourteen and that YWMIA officers "should not solicit the attendance of girls already enrolled in the Primary."[16]

An activity-oriented program was then created to interest the twelve- and thirteen-year-old girls, called the Mi-Kan-Wees or Pathfinders, which would use Indian symbols, words, and costumes as part of its program. The girls recorded their "credits" by embroidering symbols on long felt strips, called Nankos, with colorful Indian beads. The Seagull name was given to the eleven-year-old girls; with the end of Religion Classes and the subsequent stress on gospel-oriented lessons for the Primary, members of the general board felt that the name Seagull, with its connotation of service, was appropriate. Ten-year-old girls were still called Bluebirds, but the nine-year-olds, who had been Zeegees, or Zion's Girls, the year before, were renamed Larks. This entire group of girls was named Home Builders. "There is something very significant about the choice of bird names for each of these groups," noted the Primary Handbook for 1930, "for the bird song and the bird flight always typify uplift, a soaring of ideals. As mortals we rise according to the soaring of ideals."[17] Each group had its own songs, symbols, and credits to earn. Larks wore a headband with a felt candle and the words "Love lights the way." A white crown with three bluebirds on it and a multicolored headband with a white seagull on it were worn by the Bluebirds and Seagulls respectively. Home, health, religious, and cultural lessons and activities formed the Home Builder program.

Boys of comparable age to the Home Builders were called Trail Builders (the name that had previously been assigned to the ten- and eleven-year-old boys). The nine-year-old boys (previously Zeebees) were called Blazers, the ten-year-old boys, Trekkers, and the eleven-year-olds, Guides. The boys completed assigned activities along four trails known as S.H.S.K. (pronounced *shisk*), which stood for Spirituality, Health, Service, and Knowledge. The requirements to receive awards in these areas were designed to develop good habits:

1. Enlist a new member.
2. Recite scriptural passages.
3. Plant a flower or vegetable garden.
4. Take part in a play.
5. Play games or tell stories to smaller children.
6. Perform sanitary tasks two hours weekly one month, e.g., swat flies, clean yard.
7. Make a fly catcher.
8. Drink four glasses of water daily for one week, and sleep with windows open.
9. Retire at 9 P.M. five nights one week, pleasantly.[18]

The eight-year-old boys and girls who met together were still called Zeebees and Zeegees. The seven-year-olds were called Group Two, the six-year-olds, Group One, and the four- and five-year-olds, Beginners.

In 1930 the board decided to develop the lessons from the Articles of Faith in order to emphasize theological beliefs, and Articles of Faith cards were printed for each child. Activities were still part of the program, but they were subordinated and integrated into the weekly lesson. In 1933 the board decided to divide the year into four quarters, "the major assignment being the religious instruction which carried through the nine months, and the minor assignment, the leisure-time activities, which comprise the activity for the three summer months."[19] This gradual subordination of leisure-time activities sponsored by the Primary was carried one step further in 1934 when the twelve- and thirteen-year-old girls were transferred to the YWMIA and the activity-oriented Mi-Kan-Wee program was discontinued.

While agreeing that the boys and girls of the same age should belong to the same organization, the Primary was reluctant to see the children of an age group once in its charge now participating in nighttime programs. The First Presidency finally ruled that the girls should be assigned to the MIA, and the MIA, acknowledging the reservations of the Primary, responded that "we realize that our responsibility in seeing that these girls are protected is a great one."[20]

May Anderson, in presenting the decision to her board, emphasized that in defending the Primary's position, "principle and the welfare of the children had been the only consideration." But since a fundamental principle of the gospel is obedience, she reminded the board that "every member with a testimony of the Gospel would recognize that the President of the Church had both the right and the inspiration to direct the affairs of the Church."[21] The board voted unanimously to accept and support the decision of the First Presidency.

The *Children's Friend* had always reflected the changes in age groups and curriculum; from its beginning in 1902 the magazine had been essentially a lesson bulletin for officers and teachers. At the same time, general board members had discussed their hopes of seeing the *Children's Friend* become primarily a magazine for children. The first Primary handbook was not printed until 1930, and until then the magazine was the only organ for dispensing advice, lessons, supplementary activities, and special programs. By 1906 the magazine had begun to include stories and activities for children. Gradually a few photographs and simple line drawings were added, and in 1924 the general format was altered to make the magazine more attractive, especially to the children who by then had become a major audience for the publication. Larger and more frequent illustrations were included to attract the youngsters' attention, including such regular cartoon features as "Zippe-Zip."

The depression of the 1930s resulted in diminished subscriptions. To reduce costs, the number of pages was decreased and the use of color was restricted. A number of plans for increasing subscriptions were also discussed, including the publication of two magazines, one for teachers and one for children. A magazine more exclusively aimed at children might attract more readers. This plan was vetoed by the First Presidency, but the lessons were removed from the magazine in 1933 and published in separate bulletins. More drawings and special features, such as paper dolls, were added, but a number of pages were still devoted to Primary business: notes to officers, organists, music and play leaders; training lessons; and special programs. Mission lessons were included again in 1939, and in the late 1930s supplementary material for all lessons was added, since lesson bulletins were not necessarily published each year. The original goal of a magazine solely for children was not achieved during this period.

No matter how well-planned the curriculum material for various age groups or how attractive the stories and activities in the magazine, the critical factor in Primary work always remained the quality of instruction in the various local associations. The ongoing challenge had always been to instruct inexperienced women in the rudiments of teaching. Between 1919 and 1928 the teacher training program of the Church had been administered centrally, first by the Correlation Committee and then by the Church Board of Education. But after 1928 teacher training programs were again controlled by the various organizations within the Church so that specialized training could be given to workers in each group.

Primary workers were still encouraged to attend the weekly teacher training meetings held in most wards each Sunday morning by the Sunday School. Young girls who had just graduated from Primary and other inexperienced women were often called by the ward bishop to take this training course. Primary organizations were encouraged to allow these newly trained teachers to practice teaching during the summer months, then to enlist them in Primary work the next fall.

In addition, each Primary stake board was to appoint a supervisor of teacher training to work with members of the stake board, who were in turn to include teacher training work in the monthly stake union meetings attended by teachers from local ward Primaries. Lessons that dealt more specifically with challenges encountered in teaching children were prepared by the general board. Some lessons were based on teacher training texts written during the 1920s by Howard R. Driggs and Adam S. Bennion, noted Utah educators, and others dealt with the psychology and learning stages of children. Such lessons and teaching helps were also published in the *Children's Friend.* A large proportion of the first *Primary Handbook* published in 1930 dealt with such topics as lesson presentation, storytelling, and dramatization, as well as learning characteristics and stages of development of the various age groups.

Besides teacher training, monthly union meetings sponsored by stake Primary boards were centrally important for dispersing information. Since there was little direction from a central board during the nineteenth century, stake boards had been an important source of supervision and program innovation. By 1930, however, the stakes were looking to the general board as the source of the entire program and to themselves as liaisons between the general board and ward workers. The monthly union meeting was the chief tool for transferring the programs to the wards.

Stake boards usually consisted of the presidency, secretary-treasurer, chorister, organist, librarian, play leader, handwork leader, and age-group leaders. At the monthly meetings these stake leaders gave the ward workers help in the following areas: record keeping, music, maintaining a library, teaching recreational activities and handwork, teacher training, and presenting lessons. Stake leaders also visited local associations and assessed their needs and problems, and they helped to plan the annual stake conventions attended by members of the general board from Salt Lake City.

In 1930 twenty-four members of the general board were assigned to committees corresponding to the areas of supervision of stake board members. Most of the members were women who had served with Louie B. Felt. Not only did they visit annually the more than one hundred stakes, but they also began visiting many of the mission areas, especially along the western coast of the

United States. In addition, they planned an annual conference of the Primary Association in June of each year. Originally general Primary conferences had been held semiannually to correspond with general conference, but by 1930 they were held annually in conjunction with the MIA. Stake board members were expected to attend and ward workers were invited. Special pageants were presented and specific help was given in all areas of the Primary program. In addition, one meeting for Primary workers was still held in connection with the general conferences in April and October. Institutes for individual stakes were often planned by the general board, and board members made special visits to wards and stakes at the invitation of their officers.

The ongoing round of visiting as well as the planning of several extended central meetings each year were not the only responsibilities of the general board members. Their interest in the welfare of children led them into a variety of special projects. They supported Church leaders in campaigns against alcohol and tobacco and in beautification projects in the community. They continued to support legislation aimed at helping children, and certain board members were assigned to keep abreast of pertinent laws being considered. They continued their interests in social welfare, maintaining membership, for example, in the Utah and the National Conference of Social Work. Primary social work was largely in the form of campaigns for more recreation and better nutrition and health practices. They cooperated with the Relief Society in this respect—the Relief Society to improve home conditions and the Primary to provide medical care for sick children. In the late 1930s they cooperated in a Churchwide census to help find children they should be serving and to identify needs.

With all these responsibilities, the work of the twenty-four board members was exhaustive and exhausting. It was not until 1938 that they first considered the possibility of asking non-board-members to help write lessons. One board member, Marion Belnap Kerr, who wrote the lesson material for all of the age groups for many years, recalled the challenges of that assignment:

89

When our oldest child was eight months old, I was called to write the lesson department of The *Children's Friend*. At first this seemed an impossibility, but with the encouragement of my husband, my brother, who was living at my home then, Louie B. Felt and May Anderson, I undertook the work, and continued it for over eighteen years....

The *Children's Friend* and our family were co-operators. To have the copy ready for the press each month, to get the galley and form proofs read, meant less sleep for the mothers and a simple life at home. Home came first, and Primary work second. Two jobs to do meant that foods were cooked and served in a simple manner, clothing was sewed without the frills and furbelows so dear to every feminine heart, so washing and ironing could be cut to the minimum. Each day the most important things were done first. Joy in doing for the children of the Church was a good substitute for many personal desires.[22]

Some single or childless women devoted similar years of their lives to the work of the general board. Because of the scope of Primary work by the 1930s, such work was demanding and time consuming, but for the women it was a calling from God "to instill faith into the hearts of the children by means of week-day religious instruction, to help them in their leisure time activities, to safeguard the health of every child with whom we come in contact and to assist little children with sick bodies to become strong and well, that we all may rejoice together in glorifying our own lives and praising our Father who created us."[23]

Another responsibility that had always rested squarely on the shoulders of Primary workers was keeping the organization financially independent and solvent. The *Children's Friend* had been authorized by the First Presidency on the condition that the women keep it out of debt. Louie B. Felt had pledged her home as collateral, and the women had managed to make the magazine pay for itself from the beginning. The hospital was another ambitious project. Until 1929 the hospital was financially independent, and though the Church contributed some funds for its upkeep after that date, Primary pennies and contributions in kind from Primary children and friends kept the need for such support to a minimum. The importance of donations was demonstrated in 1932 when superintendents of the three Latter-day Saint hospitals in Ogden, Salt Lake City, and Idaho Falls, Idaho, suggested to the Presiding Bishopric that the children in the LDS Children's Hospital should be transferred back into the general hospitals to simplify health care. The women defended the importance of "the loving mother heart" in their hospital, which was "a combination of hospital, home, school, and church." But they also pragmatically argued that the per diem cost of care in the Primary hospital was lower because of voluntary contributions. "One cannot easily feature the contributions in addition to monies of all kinds of food supplies, bedding, clothing, etc."[24] The Presiding Bishopric allowed the children to stay in the Primary hospital "in view of the fact that the cost per patient would probably be more than the present cost...and that the transfer to the L.D.S. Hospital would cause the Primary Association to lose interest in the treatment of the children; and that in a short time no doubt the cost of the maintenance of the children would fall entirely on the Church...."[25]

Funds for the *Children's Friend* and the hospital were always maintained separately from the general Primary fund. Other general board expenses, such as visiting the stakes and holding the annual June conference, were defrayed from the nickel fund instituted in 1902. The wards and stakes raised money for their own needs by sponsoring fairs, entertainments, and pageants.

By the late 1930s, the whole problem of escalating financial demands on ward members because of the ever-growing needs of all of the auxiliaries required a reconsideration of the problem. Each auxiliary was asked to submit a plan for consolidating its needs under a single ward budget administered by the bishop. The Primary had some reservations about this plan. The practice of having children earn and contribute money for their own programs had always been considered fundamentally important in teaching them the meaning of service. The Primary asked that the *Children's Friend* and the birthday penny collection and other hospital contributions not be a part of the ward budget. The hospital was a sentimental favorite among non-Mormons as well as Mormons, and the general board feared that including these funds in the ward budget might decrease the amount collected as well as lessen the personal impact on the giver, the same arguments they had used in 1932. Their requests were granted, though the general fund (now an annual ten-cent collection) and money for books, supplies, and recreational materials were included in the ward budget.

The decision to have the finances for all of the auxiliaries collected and dispersed through the bishop illustrated a continuing trend that had been evident in the Church since early in the century. The Primary was not the only organization that had grown in size and scope during these years. The overlapping of interests and responsibilities among the various groups was inevitable, as was the resulting competition. The ongoing effort to correlate and consolidate the work of all of the auxiliaries was therefore critically important.

Primary leaders as well as other auxiliary workers in the Church were periodically given new assignments by priesthood leaders or asked to defend a certain course of action they had pursued. President May Anderson—or Superintendent Anderson, as she later chose to be titled—and other board members who had been intimately involved in shaping the contours of the Primary organization were at times understandably protective of the status quo. When the Religion Classes were discontinued, they were willing to assume the added responsibility for religious as well as ethical education, but were reluctant to diminish their longtime commitment to leisure-time activities. They had hoped that the twelve- and thirteen-year-old girls would remain in Primary, but they accepted the opposite decision gracefully and faithfully. They were pleased to keep the *Children's Friend* and the hospital as Primary-sponsored projects. In every instance when changes were suggested, the women were willing to defer to a decision based on the needs of the Church as a whole.

By the end of the 1930s the need to simplify was expressed more and more frequently from many different segments within the Church. The new ward budget plan that relieved individual Primaries from the pressures of raising money demonstrated a response to this sentiment. No matter how dedicated women were to their responsibilities to teach the gospel to the children, meeting all of the expectations of the Primary program was demanding and time-consuming. And sometimes the overall goal could be lost in a flurry of activities. A summary of suggestions from stake and ward workers after the annual round of local stake conventions in 1939 revealed a need for "more inspiration and less teacher-training work" and "fewer projects because they interfere with the lesson work." In response, the general board concluded that "with this report as a basis, it seems the greatest need might be met by more stress on Spirituality (or the WHAT and WHY we teach rather than the HOW)."[26]

That fall the president of the Missionary Home in Salt Lake City reported to the general board some suggestions missionaries had given regarding the Primary. They felt the need for a closer relationship between Primary activities and gospel principles. They also asked for mission lessons that would inspire non-LDS children to desire further knowledge about the gospel—too many children were interested only in Primary activities. They also felt that more spirituality in the lessons would help develop future missionaries and create in them a desire to live in conformity with Church standards.[27]

May Anderson had invested a lifetime in the Primary and was reluctant to see changes in the program she had helped design and build. She reminded her board in 1938 of "the history of the Primary Association, quoting from Sister Aurelia S. Rogers' story. She said the inspiration of the Lord had been strong with those early women who had visions of helping the whole child through

93

a program of lessons, work and play." She admonished her board members "to consider carefully before changing the program and eliminating certain activities.... Because there were objections to a certain project should be no reason for eliminating it." She suggested that programs be modified or simplified but not eliminated. For a woman who had assisted in laying the foundation and erecting the elaborate walls of the Primary edifice, it was difficult to consider changing or removing any of the carefully placed stones.

In December 1939, Sister Anderson was informed that she was to be released from her position as general president of the Primary. Although she would serve as president of the hospital board for five more years, it was very difficult for her to relinquish the Primary work that had been her life for fifty years. Now seventy-five years old, she addressed her board for the last time a week before Christmas. She suggested that the Primary offer to the First Presidency twenty thousand dollars of the surplus acquired through years of competent business management for the proposed new hospital building. She then told the board that in "fulfillment of a blessing received when but a little girl in the old country, her name had become known and respected in every hamlet in Zion." She acknowledged the hand of her Heavenly Father in this, for she felt her whole life had been guided and directed by a power other than her own. Her prayer had ever been, "Father, put my feet in the path you wish me to tread and I'll do the best I can." She finished by saying that "if she could put into their hearts her feeling of the importance of the Primary work and the Primary organization as a means of inspiring the children while young with faith in the Gospel of Jesus Christ and with right attitudes, she would feel that she had not lived in vain."[28]

Certainly May Anderson had stamped on the Primary organization her own unique personality and her vision of what was best for the children's welfare. She was a direct, candid woman with single-minded purpose and, as one associate put it, "it bothered her not at all if her plan was inconvenient for the teachers or difficult for the parents. If she was convinced that a course of action was best for the children, inconvenience concerned her not at all."[29]

A note written by an admirer several years after her release as Primary president is perhaps a fitting tribute to a strong-willed, dedicated, and loving woman. "After our class discussion, a week ago Sunday, my thoughts turned your way," he wrote, continuing:

I recalled all the people I knew who had "multiplied and replenished the earth" with little regard to life's purposes— and I was not exempt from review. Then I thought of you and the intelligent, loving devotion you had given to the creative life of the souls of other people's children. And I wished to express my respect and appreciation for you in the genuinely divine role you have chosen to play in life.[30]

Primary children and officers and teachers, Primary general conference, June 1914

Chapter Six

The Transition Years

In December 1939 Bryant S. Hinckley received a call from the Presidency of the Church informing him that his wife, May, had been chosen to be the new general president of the Primary. When he told her of the call "she cried pitifully and said she could not do it. All night she wept about it." He recalled, "I had to plead with her to try it. She very reluctantly consented to do this."[1] Brother and Sister Hinckley had recently returned from presiding over the Northern States Mission. Sister Hinckley, who had previously filled a mission of her own and had served as Granite Stake YWMIA president, had had almost no experience in Primary work, but on January 1, 1940, she assumed her new duties as the third general president of the Primary.[2]

The release of May Anderson ended sixty years of Primary history that had transpired under the supervision of only two women. Louie Bouton Felt and May Anderson had been the architects of the association, which by 1940 fully displayed the design they had envisioned. The Primary provided weekday religious lessons and supervised recreation for a hundred thousand children under the direction of more than eighteen thousand officers and teachers. Sister Hinckley's reluctance to accept the new assignment was understandable.

May Green Hinckley was born May 1, 1885, in Brampton, Derbyshire, England, to William and Lucy Marsden Green, the eighth of their ten children. Her mother's family had joined the Church in 1841, the first converts in Old Brampton, but her father was not a member. Lucy Green had always longed to emigrate to America, as her mother had previously done, and she had managed to save a little money from household expenses to begin sending her older children to join her mother in Utah.

Finally, when May was six, Lucy made the difficult decision to leave her husband and take her remaining children to Utah, where she could join her older children and other family members. Lucy Green lived only two years after arriving in Salt Lake City, and May was obliged to make her home for the next few years with one or another of her married brothers and sisters and with other relatives, most of whom lived in the Granite Stake. On her own initiative she augmented her childhood education with studies in business and accounting, and as a young woman she became the first manager of the business office of the Salt Lake Medical Clinic, an exceptional achievement for a woman at that time. She held this position for eighteen years.

In 1907 she was called to serve a mission to the Central States, and when she returned she worked in the MIA program of the Forest Dale Ward, Granite Stake. She was later appointed president of the stake YWMIA. During her twelve-year term she inaugurated a program for the young women of her stake that was later adopted by the general board of the YWMIA as the Gleaner Girl program.

In 1932 she married Bryant S. Hinckley, a widower with five of his children still at home. She accompanied her husband to Chicago in 1936 when he was called to preside over the Northern States Mission. Brother Hinckley appreciated the excellent work she did in the mission field. "She spent a week in Wisconsin," he recalled, "doing missionary work in one of the hardest cities in the mission. It was surprising what she could do. The people of the mission came to adore her, and the women followed her like children following their mother."[3] Just a few months after their return Sister Hinckley was called to the general Primary presidency. May Green, now May Hinckley, seemed able to manage both young people and older ones—but the call to preside over a hundred thousand little Saints was overwhelming.

In choosing her counselors Sister Hinckley turned to two

friends of forty years' standing. She selected as her first counselor Adele Cannon Howells, her former counselor in the Granite Stake YWMIA. Adele and David P. Howells had long made their home in Los Angeles, California. Now, a widow of barely one year, Sister Howells moved to Salt Lake City with her three children to accept the call to support her friend. Like May, she had had little experience in Primary work.

Janet Murdoch Thompson left the general Relief Society board to serve as Sister Hinckley's second counselor. The only one of the new presidency with Primary experience, she had served as president of the Twentieth Ward Primary for thirteen years and in the presidency of Ensign Stake Primary before moving into Relief Society work. The three friends were delighted to be together again. "It seems almost like a dream to be walking with [them] again through the church buildings," Sister Howells recorded in her diary.[4]

Though unfamiliar with the Primary program herself, Sister Hinckley surrounded herself with experienced and well-trained board members. She retained fifteen members from Sister Anderson's board and added three new ones. Most of the board members had had educational training and teaching experience, and many had had years of Primary service. Grace Wahlquist was a teacher of domestic arts and handiwork; Jessie Schofield, a graduate of the National Recreation School in New York, was superintendent of the Salt Lake City Recreation Department; Jennie Campbell, who received a master's degree from Columbia University in New York, was director of elementary education for Utah. New appointee Fern C. Eyring had studied at the University of Wisconsin, Chicago University, and Columbia University, and had taught at the Brigham Young University; Olga C. Brown, a world traveler, had taught at Utah State University and served as supervisor of health education in the Ogden City Schools and as director of the Girl Scouts in Salt Lake City.

The educational expertise of these women was brought to bear on the programs of the Primary. In January 1941, board member

Jennie Campbell "directed a discussion relative to the background and study of childhood characteristics as preliminary work for setting up new lesson standards." [5] Since most of the board members were involved in writing lessons for the various age groups, a uniformity of standards and a basic understanding of age-group characteristics were important factors in developing lesson and activity material. Vera Wahlquist of the teacher training committee also instructed the board in the principles of teacher training, and all board members contributed to developing the concepts for the teacher training lessons. When Sister Hinckley took office, the teacher development program of the Primary used the book *Fundamental Problems in Teaching Religion* by Adam S. Bennion, a local educator and later an apostle of the Church. One chapter appeared monthly in the *Children's Friend.* In 1943 the teacher training lessons for all auxiliaries appeared in the *Instructor,* organ of the Sunday School, but the Primary continued to print specific helps for its teachers in the *Children's Friend.* The Primary also enjoyed an informal association with the local and national Association for Childhood Education through the membership in that organization of many of its professional board members. The association's publication, *Childhood Education,* was regularly recommended as a source of valuable information in understanding and teaching children. Thus, both the material to be taught and the methods used to teach it were the products of experienced Primary workers and professional educators. An early handbook asserted, "Every group of Primary officers includes women of splendid ability, often unusual talent."[6] Sister Hinckley's board substantiated this claim.

The organization Sister Hinckley inherited was the product of the interests and inspired insights of her two predecessors and had been carefully nurtured under their tutelage for sixty years. At her first board meeting she told her board, "The organization is set up. The program is developed and everything is in splendid working order. It comes to us with a wonderful background, full of achievement, enjoying the confidence of the people and the authorities of the Church, a really great monument to Sister Anderson and her associates."[7]

Belying her inexperience, Sister Hinckley plunged unhesitatingly into the work of the Primary. Almost immediately after taking office she sent out a questionnaire to all Primary presidents requesting information about the effectiveness of the program. Meeting with the presidents of all the valley stakes from North Davis to Oquirrh in the south a month later, the presidency could not mistake the message they heard. "There was too much to do...."[8] The suggestions made by stake workers during the final years of Sister Anderson's administration were reiterated to the new presidency. There were too many activities and not enough time for lessons. Vera Wahlquist, who had served with May Anderson, reminded the board, as Sister Anderson had done the previous year, that the reason for the numerous projects and activities was "to meet the assignment of the Primary Association to direct the leisure-time and recreational activities of the children of the Church." Moreover, she told them, many projects had been designed as a means of raising money and would no longer be necessary because of the instigation of the ward budget system. Jessie Schofield called the attention of the board to the fact that "in spite of the complaint of too much activity...Primary membership had increased."[9]

Despite these assertions, Sister Hinckley knew that changes were warranted. To May Anderson, for whom the Primary had become her life's work, change or elimination of any of the programs she had helped to develop was tantamount to a personal rebuff. It was therefore unlikely that any major modifications would occur during her administration. It took a new administration that had no personal investment in the origin of the programs to look objectively at them and assess their effectiveness in meeting the needs of children in the 1940s. The poll of Primary workers, a general movement toward more spiritual education within the auxiliaries, plus the shift within the Church in 1939 to a general ward budget to finance the auxiliary programs had all suggested that changes were in order. The need to raise funds and to provide elaborate recreational opportunities for children were no longer requisite functions of the Primary. Moreover, the world in which Primary children lived in 1940 was quite different from their world even a decade before.

World War II raged in Europe and the Church had withdrawn its European missionaries and mission presidents and families in 1939, leaving the immediate supervision of all Church functions in local hands. Primaries in most European countries were suspended altogether. In America, which did not enter the war for another two years, the world of a Primary child was filled with "Andy Hardy" and Walt Disney movies, and the radio brought him the adventures of "Jack Armstrong, the All-American Boy" and the "Lone Ranger." "Let's Pretend" entertained young listeners on Saturday mornings. *Lassie Come Home, Daniel Boone,* and *Madeline* were recommended prizewinning books. Many attractions besides the Primary competed for the leisure hours of children.

In response to the request to simplify, the board limited the year's activities to three—a ward Primary conference in the spring, a harvest festival at the end of the summer, and a Christmas party. Class work in spiritual education was to involve three Primary days each month, two for lessons and one for enrichment, with one day a month for an elective activity determined by the stake. Although these changes were a matter of degree rather than substance, they represented a shift in emphasis from a strong activity program correlated with religious instruction to a strong program of religious instruction supplemented by appropriate activities. This shift in focus was to gain momentum after World War II when commercial recreational facilities dramatically increased and children's free time became more structured in non-Church programs. The summer program, however, retained an emphasis on purposeful activity. Summer Primary in 1940 stressed citizenship training, the development of personal skills, and the acquisition and application of social graces along with skill development in arts and crafts, music, and literature. Activities designed to develop social skills included dancing, group games, and relays. Qualification of the Home Builder girls and Trail Builder boys for the Playground Activities Badge Tests, sponsored by the National Recreation Association, was integral to the summer program.

While response to Sister Hinckley's questionnaire had suggested a general retrenchment, it also revealed that Primary workers seemed generally satisfied with the age group divisions that had developed during the last ten years of Sister Anderson's term. Sister Hinckley therefore made only minor changes. The four- and five-year-olds were to be known as Group I rather than Beginners, and the six-year-olds as Group II. The Zion's Boys and Girls were divided into two age groups, the seven- and eight-year-olds, with preparation for baptism as the major theme of their lessons. The Trail Builders (nine-, ten-, and eleven-year-old boys) and the Home Builders (nine-, ten-, and eleven-year-old girls) remained the same. The lessons for the younger age groups drew models for learning Christian virtues from Bible stories and life situations, while the lessons for the older groups, based on the Articles of Faith, stressed Book of Mormon and gospel teachings. Handiwork and crafts, "intended to provide abundant, wholesome activities for the free time of the boys and girls," continued to be a major feature of the Home Building and Trail Building programs. The local harvest festival and general June conference provided opportunities for display of the children's creative talents, and unusual crafts were often featured in the *Children's Friend* or the Church Section of the *Deseret News*. The children of the Tooele (Utah) Stake Primary, for example, were featured in the newspaper in 1940 for their craft project. They had made scrapbook covers out of soft copper in which a design was imprinted and then oxidized and polished. Boys and girls worked together on the project, using their beautifully tooled book covers for Christmas gifts.[10]

Although Scouting did not become part of the Primary program for several years after Sister Hinckley's tenure, it was already beginning to challenge the Trail Building program as an attraction for young boys. On July 17, 1940, a letter was read to the

103

general board from the Portland Stake indicating a problem that many other stakes were facing. Cub Scouting was becoming popular with the young boys in that area and taking some of them away from Primary. As a means of strengthening Trail Building, in order to keep the boys interested, the board recommended to the stake that "more male leadership be provided, that the literature and uniform be made more colorful and dramatic, that training for leadership be increased, that the organization of Trail Building be strengthened, and that close cooperation with the home be maintained."[11] The board asked for direction from Church authorities about the possibility of correlating Cubbing and Trail Building, and received an official statement in April 1941 through John D. Giles, field secretary for the YMMIA and national field scout commissioner for the Boy Scout program of the Church: "We know that there is no place for cubbing in our church. We must prepare our boys for the Priesthood and cubbing does not permit any such training."[12] As either a substitute for or an adjunct to Trail Building with its concern for priesthood preparation, Cub Scouting was not acceptable to the Church at that time. Another decade and the growing popularity of Cubbing were necessary before the Church would reconsider its policy on this program.

While Sister Hinckley was consolidating the programs of the Primary on the central level, Primary itself was expanding in the mission fields. On May 29, 1941, the general board was pleased to hear the announcement of the organization of the first Primary in Alaska. The first meeting for the children was held on June 3 at 10:30 A.M. in the Elks Hall in Fairbanks. Seventeen children of the Fairbanks Branch assembled under the direction of five women and two missionaries. The Fairbanks Primary grew through its first summer session to an enrollment of twenty-one LDS children and nine non-LDS children. Although the Primary in Alaska was discontinued with the coming of World War II, this first Primary laid the groundwork for a permanent association organized in 1950. At first, the new Primary functioned only from March until November because of the darkness and intense cold of Alaskan winters. In time, however, it was set up on a year-round basis with the stipulation that Primary would not be held if the temperature went below −20° Fahrenheit.[13]

Such adaptations were essential for the success of the program in outlying areas, and Sister Hinckley was aware of the special needs of mission Primaries. Her experience in the mission field had also made her conscious of the value of mission Primaries as proselyting aids. Within a few months after becoming president, she appointed a committee of board members to write new lessons for the missions, and plans were laid for a mission songbook. The lessons continued to be printed in the *Children's Friend* for the benefit of all Primary workers. During her administration, district mission Primaries numbered 486 with 3,857 LDS children and 4,317 non-Mormon children enrolled. Because of the large number of nonmember children attending mission Primaries, the lessons dealt with Christian virtues rather than specific Mormon doctrine.

With the discontinuation of most mission Primaries during the war, the mission lessons, which were divided into just two age groups, served hundreds of home and neighborhood Primaries that developed because of wartime travel restrictions. These Primaries provided a Primary experience for thousands of children, both LDS and non-LDS, who would not otherwise have had such opportunity during the war.

World War II brought other changes to the Primary. One month after the United States entered the war in 1941, the Church announced the suspension of all auxiliary conferences, conventions, and stake leadership meetings because of government-imposed travel restrictions. To meet the challenge of keeping the program going without personal exchanges between the board and the stakes, the Primary instituted a Stake Board Quarterly Bulletin and added a "June Conference by Mail" section to the *Children's Friend*. In time the restrictions were relaxed somewhat and board members were permitted to visit local stakes where long distances were not involved. The bulletin, however, answered a need that had been expressed earlier in answers to the questionnaire for more constant contact between the general board and stake and ward leaders. Publication of the bulletin continued until 1947.

The war also affected the publication of the *Children's Friend,* since paper was rationed. By 1944 the paper shortage was acute and appeals were made to the U.S. War Production Board for additional supplies in order to continue the magazine. Elder Ezra Taft Benson represented the Church in Washington in making the appeal, which was followed up by letters of recommendation from the governor, the chief of police, and the county sheriff as to the value of the magazine. In February of that year the magazine was ready to go to press to print 30,000 copies, but paper was available for only 23,000. Elder Marion G. Romney, adviser to the Primary, sent in an emergency call to Elder Benson, and eventually the request for sufficient paper to continue publication was granted.[14]

Sister Hinckley delegated responsibility for the *Children's Friend* to her counselor, Adele Howells, who found the assignment exciting and challenging. Always looking for interesting ideas for the magazine, she devoted much time during her first years in the Primary to this assignment. She added an officers' and teachers' "Exchange Page" where ideas and suggestions for implementing programs and activities could be shared. One teacher gave some ideas for enriching Articles of Faith lessons with posters and relay games in which children had to recite the Article of Faith requested by the teacher within a certain time period. Games for parties, ideas for plays to demonstrate lesson objectives, and inspirational incidents were also submitted by Primary workers. One "Exchange Page" was devoted to histories submitted by mission Primaries from California, Canada, New England, Denmark, and South Africa.

The South African Primary, the magazine reported, began in 1932 with seven children who called themselves "Busy Bees," using as their motto, "Service Is Sweet." By 1941 the Primary group had grown to 177 children, 84 of whom were non-Mormons. Class projects were also shared. A Trail Builder teacher told of having her boys plant a pine nut in a gallon container and care for it until it became a fledgling pine tree, the Trail Builder symbol. Another had her boys fashion decorative lapel pins out of wood, leather, and cork, and taught them to make canvas beach bags with wooden bases, which they sold to raise money for a ward building project.

To encourage children to develop their talents and interests, Sister Howells solicited letters from them describing their hobbies. A little eight-year-old boy from Talmage, Utah, wrote in to say that his hobby was collecting candies. He had forty different shapes, including a candy rose fifty years old and a candy valentine twenty-five years old. Other hobbies the children wrote about were collecting rocks, buttons, and stamps, playing baseball, riding horses, and swimming. One child liked to write western stories. Sister Howells also invited the children to submit a Bible story rewritten in their own words or a story from their own family histories. A Primary girl from Lethbridge, Alberta, Canada, submitted a story about her great-grandmother. "Great-Grandmother Harvey," she wrote, "lived in Utah at the time when people were very poor. One day while she was waiting for Great-Grandfather Harvey to come in from the fields, an old gentleman came to the door. He asked her for something to eat. She answered, 'All I have is two buns and some milk for my husband's dinner.' He asked her if she would share them with him. After he had eaten, he said to her, 'You shall never want for bread again.' That very afternoon a friend gave Great-Grandmother Harvey a bag of flour, and she was never in want of bread again." Sister Howells recommended that stake scrapbooks be kept as repositories of the children's original writings to be drawn from for publication in the magazine.

Another means of stimulating creativity was to invite suggestions from the children for making items of interest and beauty for their own rooms at home, to be published in a column entitled "In Your Own Corner." In addition, "Cut-out-and-color" pages of special construction paper were inserted in the magazine so that children could create their own stories and plays. During this time the *Children's Friend* initiated the practice of honoring the president of the Church on his birthday, a feature of the magazine that continued for a number of years.

Two interesting series that appeared in the magazine were "How the Church Carries On" and "The Stakes of Zion." Church educators and historians were invited to help prepare the materials, and each issue was generously illustrated. The "Stakes of Zion" series continued for five months and presented the origins of stakes from Kirtland and Nauvoo to the newest ones organized in Canada, Hawaii, and Mexico. In commemoration of Utah's Pioneer Day, one July issue featured a collection of interesting excerpts from pioneer diaries submitted by children and workers from each stake Primary. This feature continued for over a year and provided a valuable documentation of early pioneer experiences. Its purpose was to give Primary children a sense of their own heritage and interest them in keeping their own journals. Sister Howells, who left behind her at her death eight volumes of five-year diaries, knew the value of keeping a personal record.

In board meeting in October 1942, Sister Howells made a presentation of "a lovely Dorothy Thorpe cake plate as a prize for the most valuable ideas for the '*Friend* drive.' Phyllis Leishman won it."[15] Sister Leishman's ideas evidently spurred efforts to increase the circulation of the magazine in spite of wartime restrictions on the use of paper. The magazine, however, had already established its value as an aid to Primary workers, a help to parents, and a friend to children.

The Primary continued its interest in community and government agencies that affected the well-being of children. Representatives of the board served on the Women's Legislative Council for many years, reporting the actions of the council to the board and representing the Primary's interest in children on the council. The Primary was particularly supportive of legislation dealing with crime and juvenile delinquency, issues of concern during the war years. The council also took an active interest in school board elections and decisions, which were of similar interest to the Primary.

Only months after Sister Hinckley became president of the Primary, the board discussed the possibility of presenting a memorial gift to the Farmington Ward chapel, the scene of the first Primary meeting. Several months of planning resulted in the decision to present the ward with a mural depicting the first Primary meeting, to be painted by Lynn Fausett, a Utah artist. Photographs of some of the original participants, including Aurelia Rogers, were secured, from which he painted lifelike portrayals. One year later, on August 24, 1941, the memorial service was held in the newly renovated Farmington chapel. Rulon M. Richards, a counselor in the bishopric, whose grandmother served as first secretary to Sister Rogers, conducted. Before the presentation Sister Hinckley addressed the audience. "We are here to pay honor," she said, "to the memory of that great woman, Sister Aurelia Rogers, and to put in an appropriate and enduring form something that will commemorate the work she did, something that will show our gratitude and appreciation to her, and at the same time something that will add reverence to the place where that first meeting was held.... We are grateful above all else to our Heavenly Father whose inspiration rested upon Sister Rogers and led her to take the initiative in establishing this organization."[16]

Sister Hinckley also initiated a scripture-reading program for Primary officers and teachers. This effort to spiritualize the Primary workers in the performance of their callings was suggestive of a recommitment to making Primary a spiritual experience for children. As activities and play were confined more and more to the summer months, the focus on spiritual education broadened, and the adoption of a seal in 1940 with the words "Faith and Service" clearly indicated a maturing emphasis on the faith-building aspect of the Primary program.

The theme that Sister Hinckley and her board selected for their first June conference in 1940 became the theme of the Primary Association, and appeared as such in the *Children's Friend* in August of that year. Taken from the Doctrine and Covenants, it aptly expressed the purpose of the Primary as it had come to be defined by that time: "And they shall also teach their children to pray, and to walk uprightly before the Lord." (D&C 68:28.) In addition to a theme and a seal, the adoption of Primary colors gave further definition to the objectives of the organization: red was selected to represent bravery, courage, and fearlessness; yellow to symbolize service; and blue to represent truth, purity, and a clean life. The absence of any reference to physical, cultural, or social objectives in these symbolic representations suggests that these aspects of a child's development would be subordinate to a larger, spiritually oriented purpose.

May Hinckley saw the Primary organization as an adjunct to the home, to "assist mothers in the transcendent task of training children to pray and walk uprightly before the Lord." She envisioned it as a program to "brighten the home, strengthen the hands of parents, and teach the Gospel to children during their most impressionable years."[17] Serving only three and a half years, she worked to make the Primary a partner with the home in teaching the gospel to children. She died of an unexpected illness on May 1, 1943, at the age of fifty-eight. While her service had been brief in time, it had been deep in dedication. Without diverging far from her predecessors, she nevertheless created the impetus for change and development that would be necessary to meet the new challenges, the new demands, and the new opportunities of the postwar world. Though she had little time to go far herself, with the constant support of her priesthood advisers she carefully mapped a well-charted course that enabled her successors to see the goal ahead.

As a young woman of nineteen May Green had been promised in a patriarchal blessing, "when thy mission is fairly begun thy fame shall go forth as a mother in Israel far and near." For a childless woman, the promise was verily fulfilled. She was indeed "chosen to hold positions of trust and responsibility among her people," and she met her stewardship well.

A group of Primary teachers, Spanish Fork, Utah

Surviving members of the first Primary (1878), Farmington Ward, August 1940. Front row, left to right: Romina Chaffin Robinson, Rose Walker Chaffin, Leona Rogers Stewart, Lucy Rogers Avery, Emeline Hess Bourne, Lucy Robinson Coombs. Back row, left to right: Frances Tubbs Hess, Alfred Franklin Stevenson, James Henry Robinson, Lucy Lamb Steed, Amasa L. Clark, David C. Hess, Minnie Christensen Hughes

Chapter Seven

Expanding Horizons

On Sunday, May 4, 1947, thousands of Primary children presented a special pioneer program in their wards and branches in commemoration of the arrival of the pioneers in Salt Lake Valley a hundred years before. One Salt Lake City ward Primary, West Ensign, presented a program that included more than 145 children and 20 officers and teachers. Tableaus depicting the Mormon Battalion, pioneer women and children, a pioneer home, Indians, handcarts, and the cricket and seagull incident were explained by stories and songs. The climax of the program was a tribute to the pioneer residents of the ward. Their life histories were read and then each was presented with a red carnation. At a Primary ward conference, the St. Charles Ward Primary of Bear Lake Stake presented sketches of pioneer life entitled "We are the Pioneer Children," "Petticoats," "Saved by a Song," "The Old Rag Carpet," and "Hard Times, Come Again No More." And in Bristol, England, far away from the valley in which the original events occurred, a tiny home Primary of six non-LDS children paid homage to the Utah event by devoting the activity period of a July Primary day to reading pioneer stories.

It was to be a year in which Primary children could not help becoming acquainted with the history of the founding of the Mormon colonies in Western America. Many Primaries had already begun activities earlier in the year, following the suggestion of Primary leaders to give a living memorial to the pioneers by planting a tree on church grounds or in other appropriate places. In the St. George (Utah) East Ward, the Primary planted a pecan tree on the stake tabernacle grounds. Each Primary class made a wish for the tree, and the names of all the children contributing to its purchase were written on a sheet that was placed in a bottle and buried by the tree. Another ward Primary planted a flowering hawthorne near its chapel, also preserving the names of the children in a bottle deposited near the tree. In Manhattan Ward, New York Stake, the small Primary of twenty-three children went to Central Park on a cold day in February and assisted in planting their tree, each one taking a turn with the shovel. They named it the "Primary tree" and often held summer outings nearby. Some 33,000 Primary nickels helped to build another lasting memorial at this time—the "This Is the Place" Monument located on the east bench of Salt Lake City.

In Salt Lake City the Primary's commitment to observe the centennial was unmistakable. In June the forty-first annual Primary convention featured two elaborately staged productions. On Sunday afternoon, June 15, the production "One Hundred Years of Spiritual Development" portrayed through song, spoken word, and living pictures the theme of the Primary—"And they shall also teach their children to pray and to walk uprightly before the Lord." Pantomimes depicted a mother teaching the gospel in the home, family prayer, missionary service, the first Sunday School in Utah, the organization of the Primary, the *Children's Friend,* the joy of work, and the joy of giving.

A centennial pageant, "And the Nations Shall Be Gathered unto Zion," was presented the following two nights in the Salt Lake Tabernacle. Taking its theme from the words of Isaiah—"all nations shall flow unto Zion" and "the desert shall rejoice, and blossom as the rose"—the pageant told the story of the missionaries carrying the gospel to the world. Part I depicted the Saints leaving their homeland bound for America. Part II portrayed their trials after reaching America and in pioneering from Nauvoo to the Salt Lake Valley. In Part III Mother Earth, the narrator of the pageant, introduced in one sweeping tableau a symbolic scene of the united work of the people who conquered the desert and fulfilled the prophecies of Isaiah. Hundreds of Primary children from Salt Lake

City and surrounding areas participated, wearing authentic costumes and performing dances from the many countries where missionaries had labored. The grand scale of the production left vivid and life-long impressions on the children who were part of it.

In the summer, Primary children were taken, in imagination, on the pioneer journey from Nauvoo to Salt Lake City through the lessons, stories, and activities planned for each Primary day. They learned pioneer dances and songs, braided rag rugs, built miniature log cabins, and modeled pioneers, buffalo, and Indians out of clay. They learned to cook from pioneer recipes and to make pioneer clothes, soap, and candles, and highlighted their summer activities with "around-the-block" parades. At the harvest festival, parents viewed the results of their children's summer industry. The children of the Snowflake (Arizona) Ward Primary, for example, invited all ward members to view their pioneer handiwork neatly displayed on long tables on the lawn near the chapel, and then demonstrated the pioneer songs, games, and dances they had learned.

Each cover of the *Children's Friend* during this centennial year carried a photograph of Primary children dressed in pioneer clothing and posed in authentic pioneer settings. The previous year a serialized "Child's History of the Church" had begun, and the final chapter, the arrival in Salt Lake Valley, appeared in the July 1947 issue. The children's cut-out section of the magazine featured pioneer figures, pioneer costumes, and items from pioneer life that the children could color and cut out. The magazine also featured family pioneer experiences submitted by readers along with original pioneer poems, stories, and drawings.

Spearheading the activities of the Primary during the centennial year was Adele Cannon Howells, who had succeeded May Hinckley as general president. Explaining the extensive involvement of Primary children in pioneer activities during the centennial year, she said, "Besides giving the child a knowledge of pioneer history and bringing the Church teachings closer to him, we feel that the work is filling an important role in his future life. He is getting the basis now for continued work in hobbies and pleasure activities in his later life, a thing that is constantly being pointed out as an acute need by social workers and medical authorities."[1] This philosophy became the essence of Sister Howells's vision of the Primary and underlay the innovations that she introduced during her eight-year term as president.

On July 19, 1943, after the death of May Hinckley, Sister Howells was summoned to President Heber J. Grant's office to receive the call to preside over the Primary. As she entered his office, "President Grant kissed me as he would his own daughter," she related in her diary. Sister Howells had been a life-long friend of President Grant, his daughter Dessie being one of her best friends. He had often visited in her home in California and had even spoken at her husband's funeral. Nearly every week until President Grant's death in 1945 Sister Howells took him a loaf of freshly baked bread, and she and her counselors often rode with him and Sister Grant on afternoon rides when he was recuperating from a stroke. He repeatedly told her "how important he [thought] the training of our children in Primary is" and that he had given the Primary "as a special mission" to the new advisers, Elders Harold B. Lee and Marion G. Romney, whom he appointed at the time of Sister Howells's appointment.[2] Both her informal association with President Grant as a personal friend and her formal association with him as her priesthood leader in directing the affairs of the Primary through his appointed advisers provided a source of advice, direction, and encouragement that she relied on during her years as Primary president. Elder Lee and Elder Romney accepted their assignment with the Primary as "the special mission" President Grant wanted it to be and involved themselves with every aspect of the Primary program. For twenty years these two men strengthened and supported the work of Sister Howells and her successors. Elder Romney, reflecting on his call from President Grant to become an adviser, told Primary workers at their conference in 1948: "He sent his car for me and had me come up to his home. It was in the closing years of his life and he was pale.... He just looked beautiful as he lay on his bed there and told me that he wanted me to assist Brother Lee as an adviser to this great Primary organization.... He then said: 'The Lord gave us a revelation, a revelation about teaching the children.... We have 125,000 of them in the Church.'"

The Primary advisers echoed this concern for the children of the Church in their admonitions to Primary workers, who translated it into workable programs. In an address at the April 1949 Primary conference, Elder Romney said: "You have no conception of the power you can wield in the training of the children for righteousness in the world." Urging the sisters to recognize their basic responsibility to teach the fundamental principles of the gospel to the children so that they might take their proper place in the kingdom, he concluded, "With us, my beloved sisters, it must be the building up of the Kingdom of God or nothing."

After President Grant had set Adele Howells apart as the fourth general Primary president, she recorded in her diary that she "felt lifted up in spirit and ready to go ahead with the work as never before." She selected as her counselors LaVern Watts Parmley, who had served as second counselor to Sister Hinckley, and Dessie Grant Boyle, a member of the board and girlhood friend of Sister Howells.

Adele Cannon was born January 11, 1886, in Salt Lake City, Utah, the eldest child of George M. and Marion A. Morris Cannon. She was educated in the public schools of Salt Lake City, graduating from the LDS High and Business School in 1903. After her graduation in 1909 from the University of Utah, she taught English at the LDS College and, briefly, in Oakley, Idaho. She returned to the University of Utah to study physical education, and later she became a physical education instructor at the Deseret Gymnasium in Salt Lake City and was associated with the Salt Lake City recreation department. In 1913 she wrote an article on the playground movement for the *Young Woman's Journal* in which she traced the beginnings of the movement and its development in Salt Lake City.[3]

On March 12, 1913, Adele Cannon married David P. Howells

and left with him for San Francisco, where he attended law school. Following a successful business career that took them all over the world, the Howells made their home in Los Angeles, where David Howells served as bishop in two wards and Sister Howells was active in Relief Society and YWMIA work. There she raised her three children, Paul, Frances, and Barbara.

In 1936 Sister Howells submitted a series of articles to the *Improvement Era* under the title "From the Diary of a Bishop's Wife," describing the varied and interesting activities in which she and her husband were involved. Bishop Howells died suddenly in March 1939, and though the couple had planned to make California their permanent home, Sister Howells returned to Salt Lake City to serve in the Primary presidency when called by her friend May Hinckley a few months later. Like her predecessor, she had had little experience in Primary work, but as president she brought insight and a breadth of experience and vision from her worldwide travels. She saw the value of developing cultural and artistic skills in children as well as promoting their spiritual education, and for that reason utilized the summer quarter of Primary as a time of creative experience for them. She broadened the horizons of the Primary as an organization, involving it in projects that went beyond its own programs.

The *Children's Friend,* which was her first assignment as counselor to Sister Hinckley, provided the vehicle through which many of Sister Howells's ideas could be implemented, and it became a popular medium in which Primary children could express their ideas, interests, and artistic talents. Sister Howells established several new features in the magazine when she was counselor and editorial board member; after becoming president and editor, she added a page for the names and addresses of children seeking pen-pals and a "Be Kind to Animals" column. Children were encouraged to join the "Be Kind to Animals" Club sponsored by the magazine and to submit ideas for caring for animals and interesting stories and poems about their pets. It was a popular page with children and elicited many responses each month.

A dream of Sister Howells that began as early as 1942 did not become a reality until four years later. In 1942 she suggested to the board a plan for a children's radio program sponsored by the Primary. Through the *Children's Friend* the board had been consistently recommending to the children good radio programs, such as "Story Telling Time," "The American School of the Air," and "Let's Pretend." But a radio program of its own would enable the Primary to bring to young listeners good quality programming, furthering Primary objectives. In 1943 Sister Howells met with Church officials and community members who worked with children or were involved in broadcasting, and presented the idea to them. It was not until June 15, 1946, however, that the first broadcast of "Children's Friend of the Air" was presented to its many listeners in Salt Lake City and nearby areas. The fifteen-minute program presented stories from the *Children's Friend* adapted for radio dramatization by Olive Milner and directed by Becky Thompson. A number of children participated over the years, playing the various characters in the stories. For the first six months children were encouraged to submit original poems to be read on the program. Later they were asked to bring their hobbies and pets and talk about them over the radio. During 1947, the centennial year, one program a month was devoted to pioneer stories.

When "Children's Friend of the Air" was a year old, the station that sponsored it was one of 360 stations from all networks to submit a publicity book to the Radio Publicity Contest in Atlantic City. Included in the publicity book were two pages of pictures about the radio program, including some from its first anniversary party, one of its floats in the Salt Lake City Christmas parade, and some of a *Children's Friend* hobby display featured in a window of ZCMI, a Salt Lake City department store. The presentation won second prize in the national contest.

Only a month after television came to Utah in 1948, the Primary sponsored a second media program, "Junior Council," a weekly half-hour television show that originally featured a panel of Primary children answering questions submitted by the studio audience or by readers of the *Children's Friend*. The questions were both serious and comic, dealing with such subjects as baby-tending, parents, school, foods, sports, etiquette, and friends. One child asked: "I like all my teachers but one. I am very unhappy about this. What can I do to like the teacher?" Another wondered how she could be happy when doing the dishes. One girl wanted to know "why mothers don't have time to tell you things," and another complained about having to learn poetry in school and wondered why it was necessary. The panel answered the questions giving a child's point of view to the pressing issues. Later, the program altered its format to include demonstrations of arts, crafts, hobbies, scouting skills, and "how-to" projects by Primary children. Home Builder girls explained how to make shadow boxes, holiday candles, and embroidered articles. Scouts demonstrated knot-tying and campfire-building. The program also featured members of the *Children's Friend* "Be Kind to Animals" Club, who brought their pets and explained how to care for them. Special guests presented puppet shows, talent acts, short plays, and even parades. Others gave lessons in how to draw, how to enjoy music, and how to make unusual gifts. Network television programming soon eliminated most locally sponsored programs, and "Junior Council" eventually gave way to nationally produced children's shows, as did its sister program "Children's Friend of the Air." But during their years of production, these two programs provided an outlet for the creative talents of hundreds of Primary children and brought good children's programming into the home. They also stretched the boundaries of the Primary's concern deeper into the community and established a standard of achievement for Primary children everywhere.

In 1949 a request was issued for a set of pictures illustrating the Book of Mormon. Having moved the Primary conference from June to April the previous year, Primary leaders were able to meet with mission presidents attending the general conference sessions. The first year the Primary met with twenty mission presidents and their wives, who reported on the Primary in their missions, followed by an exchange of ideas and suggestions. The next year, during this discussion period, a mission president indicated the need in his mission for Book of Mormon pictures. Other mission presidents concurred, and the names of several artists were mentioned as possibilities for painting the much-needed pictures. In March 1950 Sister Howells and Mary Jack, managing editor of the *Children's Friend,* visited a local book publishing company to see the work of an artist who was interested in doing Book of Mormon paintings, and later that year Sister Howells indicated in her diary that she was actively trying to secure some Book of Mormon pictures that she wanted to be printed first in the *Children's Friend.*[4]

Arnold Friberg was the artist finally selected to do the paintings. He had moved to Utah in 1949 as a convert to the Church. He was commissioned by the Primary general board to paint the Book of Mormon series as a commemorative feature of the fiftieth anniversary of the *Children's Friend* in 1952. The first painting did not appear until the January 1953 issue, and the others, twelve in all, appeared irregularly for the next eight years. The story of the Book of Mormon, prepared for children by board member Mary Pratt Parrish, ran for four years in conjunction with the pictures. The paintings have been reproduced many times for use in Book of Mormon curricula for the auxiliary programs of the Church. In 1953 the National Offset-Lithography Competition gave its award for the best magazine insert of the year to the *Children's Friend* for the Book of Mormon paintings.

Adele Howells had set as a goal for the magazine 50,000 subscriptions for its jubilee year. The goal was not only met but exceeded, with a final count of 72,000 subscriptions.

While the *Children's Friend* occupied much of the interest of Sister Howells, she did not neglect the other responsibilities of her office. Though none of the age groupings were changed during her term, she supervised several revisions of lesson manuals and new editions of the officers' and teachers' handbook. While the Primary had begun to enlist the help of Institute of Religion leaders and educators, such as Lowell Bennion and T. Edgar Lyon, to write lessons for the older age groups, board members were still assigned to write all of the other class lessons. Like Marion Belnap Kerr, who for eighteen years had written the lessons when they were published in the *Children's Friend,* Mary Parrish, assigned to write the manual for the seven-year-olds, found it a taxing and yet valuable experience. Though she was an accomplished writer, this assignment required special skills and a great deal of preparation. Three months went by before she could write a word. Then, after finally writing eight of the thirty-six lessons, she found herself dissatisfied with them and knew she had to start again.

Seeking spiritual guidance, she took counsel from the scriptures and from Elder Harold B. Lee, Primary adviser, who said to her, "Sister Parrish, you've been asked to write a lesson book; now go home and do it!" Then putting his arm around the weeping board member, he added, "Sit down and I'll give you a blessing." He promised her that the manual would be written, and that it would be written by the power of the Holy Ghost. Soon thereafter the idea came to her for the first lesson, and without hesitation she wrote it all. It met immediate approval from her committee. The next few lessons were disappointing, but, trying again, she stayed up all one night, rewriting them. "Then the miracle happened," she said. "For the next two weeks I felt I was just the scribe. I wrote as if I were being dictated to. As one idea unfolded, another one came. Truly Brother Lee's prophecy that the book would be written by the power of the Holy Ghost was fulfilled." She remembered long afterwards a passage from a dramatic production that she had seen during that time: "If knowledge and skill cannot do a thing, faith can." Her experience had proved to her the truth of those words.[5]

After her manual was completed, Sister Parrish felt strongly that the women of the board, who were close to the children and knew their needs, should write all of the lessons. One board member was reluctant to put her work up against that of one of the Institute teachers who was writing some of the lessons. But

Sister Parrish remonstrated: "You can write a book better than [he] because you know more about these girls than he does." Affirming what early-day Primary workers had always known—that women knew best how to teach children—the board members took over all of the lesson writing, and as a result the lessons assumed a continuity and perspective more reflective of the women's purposes, determined long before, for the Primary children. These women who were called to direct the affairs of the Primary from earliest days were but ordinary people, some more trained in special educational skills or more experienced than others, but together they performed a service that always seemed to be greater than the sum of their efforts.

Along with writing lesson manuals, board members continued to write helps for teaching the lessons. In 1949, in response to a request that all of the teacher training lessons be issued at the beginning of the year, the first teacher training manual of the Primary was published. For the next twenty-one years a new manual was published every year. More than seventy years before, in response to a similar need for materials and help, Eliza R. Snow had compiled a hymnbook, a tune book, and a poem and recitation book, and had written several gospel catechisms for children. Now this method of teaching was sadly out-of-date. A section from a "Book of Mormon Catechism," originally published in the *Juvenile Instructor* in 1886 for the Sunday School, was reprinted in the 1950 teacher training manual with the question: "Would you like to keep the interest of a group of children with such a lesson?"

1. Q. What is the Book of Mormon?
   A. The sacred history of ancient America.
2. Q. By whom was it written?
   A. A succession of ancient prophets who inhabited the continent.
3. Q. On what was it written?
   A. On plates which had the appearance of gold.
4. Q. What kind of characters were engraved on the plates?

    A. Reformed Egyptian characters on both sides of each plate.

5. Q. In what were they concealed?
    A. A stone box strongly cemented together which was placed beneath the soil.

6. Q. How large was the box?
    A. Sufficiently large to admit of a breast-plate, such as was used by ancient warriors, and the Urim and Thummim, together with the plates.

7. Q. After Joseph Smith had found the plates, opened the box and was viewing the contents, who appeared to him?
    A. The angel Moroni who had previously visited him and who was surrounded by the glory of God.

8. Q. Did any other personage appear to him?
    A. Yes, the prince of darkness with his hosts.

9. Q. Why was he shown the two powers?
    A. That he might thereafter know them and not be influenced or overcome by the evil one.[6]

Very few present-day teachers would be willing to struggle through the rote and drill method of teaching used a century ago. Yet many hundreds of little Saints learned gospel principles through just such a method and the patience of devoted sisters willing to teach them.

During Sister Howells's tenure, the Primary teacher trainer was not a special office in the ward Primary organization, but rather a secondary assignment of either a counselor or teacher. She presented a lesson once a month in ward preparation meeting. Continuing to stress the principles of progressive education, the Primary viewed its teachers as guides helping each child to learn and understand gospel concepts according to his or her individual differences rather than schoolmasters drilling facts into a child's mind.

Always receptive to current educational studies, Sister Howells and her board participated in child education conferences held at local institutions and brought noted educators in to acquaint Primary workers with new methods of understanding and teaching children.

While gospel principles had become the major course work of the Primary, leisure-time activities were still the emphasis of the summer program. Not all Primaries, however, were year-long associations, many wards and stakes dismissing for the summer months. Knowing the value of a year-round program and Sister Howells's desire to see it adopted everywhere, Elder Lee reinforced her efforts by repeated admonitions to stake Primary leaders to utilize the entire program. At the Primary conference in 1949 he quoted from the handbook, delineating the Primary's objectives, one of which was "to supervise and direct the leisure-time activities of children." "With that in mind," he told the Primary workers, "do you not think it a travesty for the Primary ... to go on vacation in the summer when the children have the most spare time, and then resume your activities during the fall of the year when they are the busiest and have the least spare time?" A year later he was still encouraging the sisters to implement the whole program: "I would ask you to consider these things well," he said. "Whenever the work of the Lord goes on vacation, that is when the power of Satan's program is put in full play and the substitute organizations for the Lord's work have their great innings to win the Lord's people away from his Church.... There must be no vacation ... for 'those whom the Holy Ghost hath made overseers over the flock, even the Church of God.'" Summer Primary received a great spurring forward during the centennial pioneer celebration and gradually became, wherever feasible, a universally accepted part of the Primary program.

Although most mission Primaries outside the United States were suspended during World War II, the lessons for mission and home Primaries continued to appear in the *Children's Friend*. They were utilized primarily by the five hundred home Primaries that were functioning when Sister Howells became Primary president. Most of these Primaries had been established because of travel restrictions in the United States during the war. At the end of the war most of them converted to regular Primaries, and home Primaries operated only where distance or lack of children made a regular unit impractical. For example, a group of children living in one Salt Lake City ward whose homes were in a distant corner of the ward's boundaries, who attended a different school from the other children in the ward, and who were separated from the ward building by busy railroad tracks, met in the home of one of their mothers. These twelve children, ages four to eleven, were divided into two age groups and given the mission lessons out of the *Children's Friend.*

At the European Mission Presidents Conference held in July 1947, it was reported that in most countries no Primaries had been held during the war, but many were again beginning to function. Norway had organized five, Belgium and Switzerland one each, and the Netherlands nineteen. The British Mission president reported an enrollment of 281 children, only 73 of whom were LDS. These early postwar Primaries offered children of war-torn countries friendship, supervised activity, and organized religious training, which many of them had never had before. In 1948 the Berlin District Primary treated four hundred Primary children to a spring festival held at an "open-air restaurant at Krumme Lanke, not far from the mission home on the edge of a little lake surrounded by green woods." Before the festivities began, each of these wartime children was given a "generous helping of delicious pudding, the like of which they had never before seen." A program followed consisting of songs, poems, and dances. The children of the Berlin East Branch presented a play, "Liza in Fairyland." The stage had been transformed into a beautiful meadow with flowers, grass, and trees, and the children were delightfully costumed. After the program, each child was given a little cake with orange juice, another special treat for them. As they left to go home, the boys received a balloon and the girls a ribbon, presents many of them had never had before.[7] Many families joined the Church through such activities of their children in Primary.

When Primary leaders met with mission presidents at the April general conference in 1949, one of the problems they discussed was the content of lesson material. Since most of the children attending mission Primaries were non-LDS, the lessons had been based on general Christian principles rather than Mormon doctrine. It was decided at the meeting that because of the missionary value of these Primaries, LDS doctrine would henceforth be incorporated in the lessons, and the nonmember children attending them would be introduced to the principles of the gospel.

The year 1949 was pivotal in Adele Howells's administration. In addition to a new focus for mission leaders, a compilation of teacher training lessons into one annual volume, the decision to commission the Book of Mormon paintings, and a change in national policy lowering the Scouting age for boys from twelve to eleven (necessitating changes in the Trail Building program), the year also brought a long-awaited letter from President George Albert Smith to Sister Howells. After years of delay, the Primary had finally been authorized to go forward with the construction of the new Primary Children's Hospital.

The Hyde home on North Temple had outworn its efficiency as a convalescent center, and a new hospital was necessary to provide the much-needed services unavailable in the old home. On November 6, 1937, Anna Rosenkilde, superintendent of the hospital, had written a letter to President Heber J. Grant, outlining the difficulties presented by the inadequate building. She described a diptheria outbreak and the difficulty of isolating patients with the disease because of limited space. The necessity of carrying food trays from the kitchen downstairs to the patients upstairs imposed an undue hardship on the nurses. The laundry was inadequate. Sister Rosenkilde told of a fire that had broken out in the home a few years before. The nurses had had to fight their way through smoke-filled rooms to gather the babies who were then in the home. They rushed them next door to the Nurses' Home, where they were visited by President David O. McKay, who saw ten wide-eyed and frightened babies lying side by side on a big bed. She then concluded:

Are children not our most precious possessions whether they are rich or poor, whole or possessed of a broken body? I feel sure we could do a much better piece of work in a more adequate building.

When may we look for something shining and beautiful for the children? A building with plenty of sunlight, cheery walls and a nice floor for children to play on. The lovely, safe building that would warm the hearts of the good Sisters who come from the Country with their offerings for the children and say, "What would you like us to do?" Would they not feel encouraged in their efforts?[9]

Sister Rosenkilde received a direct reply from President Grant in which he pledged not only his immediate attention to the erection of a new hospital, but also two thousand dollars toward its construction. It was President Grant to whom Sister Felt and Sister Anderson had appealed when they first determined the need for a children's hospital in 1921, and it seemed appropriate that it was to President Grant that the appeal was made for the new hospital.

Anna Rosenkilde, or "Mama Rose" as the children called her, had been with the hospital since its beginning in 1922. "The hospital," she often said, "was a procession of the sick and those needing our help." Her devotion to the children best demonstrated itself in her adoption of one of them, a young boy who lost his legs through severe burns, and whom she raised to active, independent adulthood. Sister Rosenkilde, a Danish convert, immigrated to Utah in 1900 to live with a sister in Eden, northeast of Ogden. In 1904 she accompanied Elder Owen Woodruff and his family to Mexico City. When both Elder and Sister Woodruff died of smallpox, she returned to Salt Lake City with the four young Woodruff children and cared for them for many years. Later she attended Brigham Young University for a year and then entered nurses' training at LDS Hospital. During World War I she served in France with the Army Nurse Corps of the Army Expeditionary Forces. In 1922 she was appointed the first superintendent of the Primary Children's Hospital, serving for twenty-four years. She retired before the new hospital was built. She was remembered as a tireless worker who "developed a deep love for 'every stick and stone' of the children's hospital." Her work at the hospital merited the gratitude of thousands of children. "She will never be forgotten," one tribute affirmed, "by those who have come into her life's path."[10]

As a result of Sister Rosenkilde's letter, George Cannon Young, Salt Lake City architect, received a summons to Presiding Bishop Sylvester Q. Cannon's office, where he learned that he had been chosen to design the new hospital. His original plans called for construction of a fifty-bed hospital at a cost of $300,000. Several locations were examined as possible sites, and a large lot high on the north bench of Salt Lake City was finally chosen.

At a testimonial dinner given in honor of President Grant on his eighty-second birthday, November 22, 1938, business leaders of the Salt Lake City community presented him with a copper chest containing one thousand silver dollars. They suggested to him that following his usual pattern with such gifts, he give them to his favorite charity. At that time his favorite charity was the Primary Children's Hospital, and he donated the money to that cause with the injunction that since $300,000 was needed, the silver dollars should be sold for three hundred dollars each. This gesture was the beginning of a tremendous outpouring of contributions from groups and individuals through drives and campaigns that ultimately raised the funds for the new hospital.

The construction of the building was to suffer an unfortunate delay, however, with the coming of World War II and the death of President Grant. But at war's end in 1945, the cause was taken up again with enthusiasm. The unsold silver dollars were put into brass paperweights with the inscription "Primary Children's Hospital Fund" and the signature of Heber J. Grant on them, to be sold for one hundred dollars each. One group of Primary Children in Salt Lake City raised the money to buy a paperweight themselves. The Blazer boys of the McKay Ward had heard the story of President Grant and his silver dollars and decided that they wanted to contribute by buying one of the paperweights. They began by selling candy and popcorn balls at stake road shows, and soon the entire Primary joined in. At Thanksgiving, instead of contributing fruit baskets to the older people of the ward, the children contributed to the paperweight fund. At Christmas they made a large paper chimney to hold the pennies and nickels they donated. They finally raised the one hundred dollars, and at their spring Primary ward conference, they presented the paperweight to the bishop to keep in his office.[11] The sale of the paperweights eventually brought $120,000 to the hospital fund.

To involve the children beyond their contribution of birthday pennies, Sister Howells inaugurated a "Buy a Brick" campaign. Each child was asked to contribute ten cents to buy a brick for the hospital. Their response brought over $20,000, which bought 203,303 bricks and mortar. At one time, when a Primary board member was conducting a group of children through the new building, one little boy tugged at her skirt and asked, "Lady, can you tell me which is my brick?"[12]

By this time, the plans had been revised. The hospital was now to accommodate sixty beds and provide a greater range of services than originally envisioned. The groundbreaking occurred during Primary conference in April 1949. President George Albert Smith stated in his remarks at that ceremony: "I want it to be the finest building of its kind in the world."[13] President Smith also officiated at the ceremonies for laying the cornerstone in April 1950. In the box to be laid in the cornerstone were the names of donors to the Brick Fund along with other historic documents.

Many individuals who were instrumental in making the new hospital a reality did not live to see its completion in 1952. President Grant and President Smith, May Anderson and Adele Cannon Howells had all died before that time and Sister Rosenkilde had been released as superintendent. But others continued their work and assisted in making it "the finest building of its kind in the world."

Under the direction of Adele Cannon Howells the Primary Association reached beyond the lessons and activities of its weekday program. Through the use of the traditional nickel fund, little Saints had opportunity to become involved in larger Church and community projects. Like the nickel funds of early days that helped to immigrate children, build temples, pay for the visits of general board members, and publish the *Life Sketches* of the Primary's founder, Aurelia Rogers, the latter-day nickel funds bought trees planted as living memorials to the pioneers, and assisted in the erection of the "This is the Place" monument commemorating the arrival of the pioneers in the Salt Lake Valley. They helped to commission an artist to paint the memorial mural in the Farmington Ward chapel and another to paint murals on the walls of the baptistry in the new Idaho Falls Temple. And for two nickels each the children bought bricks to build their own hospital.

Adele Howells provided a model from which Primary children could learn the joy of giving of oneself. A woman of wealth, she was a generous, caring person. Bringing to the Primary the same flair with which she graced her own life, she infused the program with a vitality and a vision of possibility that touched every child. She regularly invited stake boards to meet in her home, where she could share their problems and ideas, serving lunch or refreshments afterwards. Her board members and advisers were treated to annual visits to her ranch east of Salt Lake City, where they had opportunity to ride "Primary" and "Children's Friend," two of her many horses. She often provided transportation to the Primary office for her counselors, since neither of them could drive. With the help of a devoted maid at home, she frequently invited board members and her counselors to dinner after late meetings, and many knotty problems were discussed and unraveled over the lunches that she hosted. She contributed thousands of dollars to the new hospital and sent Easter and Christmas boxes anonymously to needy families. This generous spirit was undoubtedly the force underlying her desire for Primary children to learn to share, to give, and to care for others. The murals, the monument fund, the Buy-a-Brick project, and a Hospital Remembrance Fund were all Sister Howells's ideas. But beyond their contribution of nickels and dimes, Primary children had opportunity to give of themselves in other ways. At the end of World Ward II, they were invited to gather toys and clothing for the children of Europe, collecting 122,794 articles that were packed into 3,451 cartons. And she provided for them opportunities to share their talents and creativity on their own radio and television programs and in the *Children's Friend.*

If any one theme characterized Sister Howells's administration it would be her vision of broadening the horizons of the Primary child through opportunity for community involvement and the development of natural and creative talents. Her interest in the value of creative participation as a learning process was evident in the programs she initiated. "We feel," she once said, "that a child takes a greater interest in the subject we are trying to teach him if he can take part in some creative project."[14]

While Sister Howells initiated many programs that helped shape the contour of the Primary during the eleven years she was associated with it, she was "rarely out front," as one board member remembered her. "She was always behind the scenes pushing.... she would throw out a problem to the board and let them discuss it and from the discussion drew her conclusions."[15] But there were times, she learned, when in her capacity as president she had to make final decisions herself. She recorded in her diary the advice Elder Marion G. Romney gave her when she asked him about voting on a difficult question before the board. "...as President of an organization," she wrote, "it was my duty with my counselors to obtain and hear the opinions of board members but in the final analysis I must decide what action to take according to my best judgment with the help of the Lord. I would be held responsible for that judgment." Elder Romney then told her of a time when President Wilford Woodruff felt impressed to make a decision against the advice of several of his apostles. "When he thought of doing it," said Brother Romney, "he saw light and when he thought of not doing it, he saw darkness." Sister Howells concluded, "He had to make his decision and I with God's help will make mine."[16]

For her outstanding contributions to the state of Utah, Sister Howells was elected to the Salt Lake City Hall of Fame in 1948. She was honored not only for her work with thousands of children through the Primary Association, but also for her generous donations to the Brigham Young University and University of Utah teacher training schools and for her scholarship programs for the development of art and creative skills in children. She died after a brief illness on April 14, 1951, at the age of sixty-five. Though she did not live to see the completion of some of her major projects, such as the dedication of the new Primary Children's Hospital and the jubilee year of the *Children's Friend,* Adele Cannon Howells carried the work forward for others to finish.

Primary float from an early July 24 parade

Chapter Eight

"Going Up Against a Stone Wall"

"In thinking over the problem involved I was greatly troubled as we have a momentous decision to make...."[1] The decision facing the Primary board at the beginning of 1950 that President Howells thus confided to her diary was centered on the eleven-year-old boy. The previous October the announcement had come from National Boy Scout headquarters that the Scouting age had been lowered from twelve to eleven. In the Church, Scouting was a YMMIA program, picking up the boys when they graduated from Primary at age twelve. Now the dilemma before the Primary was whether to incorporate Scouting into the Primary program or give the eleven-year-old boys to the YMMIA, as it had the twelve- and thirteen-year-old boys in 1913.

Central to the issue was the Primary's responsibility to prepare boys for the priesthood, and this factor determined the recommendation by the general Primary presidency in February 1950 that Scouting not be made a part of the Primary course of instruction. Under the Primary recommendation, the YMMIA was to have total responsibility for the Scouting program and to meet with the eleven-year-old boys in a separate session to give them their Scouting instruction. The Primary would eliminate Scouting preparation from its Trail Building program and concentrate on its major goal—training boys for the priesthood. The First Presidency approved the recommendation. An entry in Sister Howells's diary for February 21, 1950, suggests the concern and prayerful efforts that had been part of this resolution of the problem. "Brother Lee said they were pleased with what we had done on the Scouting question and that we had been prayed for by them that we should receive guidance from the Lord. He felt that we had been 'born up on the wings of prayer' which we know to be true. May God help us to finish as we have begun on this important question."

The solution arrived at in 1950, however, turned out to be but a preliminary step in the ultimate resolution of the problem of Scouting and Primary. This first step had not taken into consideration the growing appeal of Cub Scouting. Moreover, it was becoming evident that shared responsibility for the eleven-year-old boy imposed a double burden on the boy. Instead of one meeting a week he was required to attend two, and he was accountable to two leaders. Finding Scout leaders who were available to direct a daytime patrol meeting in addition to a regular patrol meeting in MIA proved to be impossible in many wards. Outside of Utah, where ward boundaries were wider and members more scattered, an extra meeting involving only a small number of boys caused additional hardship. As a result, the boys usually had to make a choice between Primary and MIA. Clearly, within only a year or two, a reassessment of the program was indicated.

Scouting was but the first of several significant challenges LaVern Watts Parmley would meet after becoming general Primary president on May 16, 1951. But she was well armed with years of Primary experience and a particular penchant for and understanding of the boys' program. She began her Primary service as a play leader in the Grant Ward before she was married and continued some years later when as a young mother she was called to the Bonneville Stake Primary board. She was given responsibility for the boys' program, which she always felt was her "specialty." In July 1941, having served three years on the stake board, she was called to the general board. Only seven months later, February 1942, Sister Hinckley asked her to fill the position of second counselor in the general Primary presidency. Sister Parmley found the call overwhelming. One of the newest members of the board, she felt unqualified for such a responsibility, and she was also concerned about her three young children at home. But when she heard her name announced as the new second counselor by Sister Hinckley in board meeting a few minutes later there was no time for remonstrance. She was beginning a service of general Primary leadership that would continue for thirty-two years.[2]

Sister Parmley's capability for leadership became apparent as she struggled with the Scouting problem just a year after becoming president. In a meeting with the First Presidency and Presiding Bishopric on May 9, 1952, she outlined the problems the Primary was having in the divided responsibility of the eleven-year-old boy. After much discussion the earlier decision was overturned. The Primary was now to assume full responsibility, adapting its program to include Scouting along with priesthood preparation. But something else was decided that Sister Parmley had not anticipated. Because of the competition Cubbing was giving to the Church, drawing boys away from Primary in many areas, the Primary was also to assume direction of Cub Scouting. President David O. McKay told of one place where Mormon boys in a non-LDS pack were invited to join the boys' choir of the church sponsoring the Cub Scout pack. The boys' choir sang on Sundays and the Mormon boys were missing their Sunday meetings as well as Primary. Reports of many such incidents had brought the First Presidency to the decision to offer Cub Scouting under Primary leadership. It was reasoned that "a boy who begins his scouting experience under the sponsorship of the Church in Cub Scouting automatically advances into the Guide Patrol and completes his Scouting and Exploring in the YMMIA. This continuity is often lost when Cub Scouts join units sponsored by other institutions."[3]

Sister Parmley's response to these two new additional assignments is understandable. "When I think of the *Children's Friend,* the Primary Hospital, and all the Primary programs," she responded, "and now to have four years of Scouting, that's a big responsibility....It's just like going up against a stone wall."[4] In characteristic manner, President McKay replied: "The wall may seem insurmountable but we cannot stand back and say there is no use trying. We can walk the distance to the wall. We are not discharging our duty until we go up to it, and when we do that there may be a hidden ladder which we have not seen, or over here there may be a door through which we can pass. If you come up against a wall, let us know."[5] Sister Parmley found many occasions to remember these words, which, she said, taught her a vital lesson that she never forgot. She also felt the reassuring support of constant priesthood leadership, which bolstered her own efforts in fulfilling the obligations of her calling.

The Primary board immediately set to work planning how the Scouting program for the eleven-year-old boys could be integrated into the Primary program. The first step was to obtain permission from the National Scout Committee for women to work in Scouting. Heretofore only the position of den mother in the Cub Scout program was open to women. Joseph A. Brunton, Jr., chief executive of the Boy Scouts of America, spent several days in Utah with the Primary officers helping organize the program. Before he left he made it clear to them that though women in the Church would be permitted to serve as leaders of the eleven-year-old Scouts, they would not be recognized as registered Scout workers with the right to titles, awards, or uniforms.

Next, the weekly Primary meeting of the Guide class had to be altered to accommodate the requirements of Scouting. The name of the Guide class was changed to the Guide Patrol, later becoming the Blazer Scout Patrol in 1975. Though nominally under the ward Boy Scout troop, it would function as an independent unit under the supervision of the Primary. The objective was still to prepare a boy for priesthood responsibility, but also to assist him in becoming a Second Class Scout. Since the Scouting program did not include specific lessons, those from the Guide class manual were utilized to continue the religious training. In addition to the lessons, the boys were taught the Scouting traditions and ideals that formed the "Scout Spirit": the motto, slogan, oath, and the twelve points of the Scout law. Many of the Christian values incorporated in these ideals complemented the spiritual lessons taught in the Trail Building program, and Scouting provided an outlet for practical application of these objectives. The activities required for advancement in Scouting replaced the activities previously included in the Guide program.

The program's first two years were largely experimental in the wards and stakes, but with the publication of the *Guide Patrol Digest* in 1957 by the Primary board, the coordination of Scouting with Primary work was clearly established and the objectives more specifically defined. The introduction to the digest, written by President McKay, states the attitude behind the coordination of the two programs: "Scouting will help '... to do better the things we have always wanted to do with and for our own boys....'"[6]

Organizing Cub Scouting offered a different set of problems. Cubbing was not to be part of the regular Primary curriculum, but would operate as a separate organization directed by a separate group of leaders under the supervision of the Primary. It is a home- and neighborhood-oriented program that provides boys supervised activity compatible with the objectives of the Primary. The pack committee, Cubmaster, and den leaders are called to their positions by the ward bishopric. Parents are oriented to the Cubbing program by the Cubmaster. The emphasis of the program is child-parent involvement, and parental cooperation is a great factor in making the program successful.

Years before, President George Albert Smith, speaking at a general Primary conference meeting in 1946, had compared the work of the Primary with that of Cub Scouting—long before the two were associated. He told the Primary workers that Scout officials had come to learn through Cubbing what Church officials had long known through the Primary Association: that women should be given the "task of laying the foundation for the education and training of boys of that age." He then declared that he felt that with women in charge of the training program of the younger boys, a more effective job of teaching was being accomplished. Six years later, when Cubbing and Trail Building joined hands, women did indeed receive a great responsibility through

139

these two programs in the teaching and training of the young boys of the Church.

In every country where there are LDS youth, the Church has desired to affiliate with and utilize the national Scouting program. Sometimes, however, that affiliation has not been possible either because of the Church's inability to qualify for a charter or because the individual national Scouting program did not meet Latter-day Saint standards or program regulations. Therefore, in 1972 the Primary general board developed an interim Scouting program to be used temporarily where national charters were unobtainable. In all foreign countries negotiations for charters are handled by priesthood representatives.

A special activity for the eleven-year-old boy was developed under Sister Parmley's leadership, emphasizing the other aspect of the youth's Primary work. That is the priesthood correlation program whereby twice a year the presidency of the deacons quorum visits the boys to instruct them on their duties as deacons and the importance of the Aaronic Priesthood. In addition to these visits, a "Priesthood Preview" is held under the direction of the stake priesthood presidency. All eleven-year-old boys and their fathers are invited to attend.

When the Primary Association became involved with the national Scouting program, it was necessary for the national organization to reassess the involvement of women in Scouting. Permitting LDS women to serve as Scout leaders was but the first step in broadening the opportunities for women to participate in Scouting, although major policy changes did not come for nearly fifteen years. The effectiveness with which the program was organized and administered under Primary women and the pressures of the women's movement undoubtedly worked together to stimulate change. Contrary to Mr. Brunton's assertion in 1953, women are now registered Scouters: they wear uniforms and insignias, serve on local and national boards, and are eligible to receive Scouting awards.

Sister Parmley, as general president of the Primary, was

honored as the first woman to participate in many aspects of Scouting under the new policy. She was called in 1967 to serve on the Religious Relations Committee of the National Boy Scouts of America, the first time in history that a woman had ever been called to a national Scouting committee. She has served on the National Cub Scouting Committee, the first woman to do so (although several women have served since), on the National Advisory Council, and on the National Program Committee. Although still only relatively few women serve on national committees, the influx of women on local levels is more dramatic, again exemplified by the involvement of Sister Parmley. She has been chairman of Area 22 of the Western Region of Cub Scouting and serves on the executive board of the Great Salt Lake Council.

When Scouting administration was first opened to LDS women, a Women's Reserve of the Boy Scouts of America was created in which they could be officially registered. With this change came a special award for women, the Silver Fawn, comparable to the Silver Beaver award for outstanding service in Scouting by men. Today there is no distinction between the service of men and women in Scouting, and both of these special designations for women have been discontinued. A trail blazer for women in Scouting, Sister Parmley has been given the Silver Beaver, the Silver Antelope, and the Silver Buffalo awards. She also received the Minute Women Award from the National Guard, the Distinguished Service Award from the Salt Lake County Medical Society, and the Region 12 Outstanding Citizen Award. In 1973 she was elected to the Hall of Fame by the Salt Lake Council of Women. Few, if any, other women in the country have given more service in Scouting than LaVern Watts Parmley. She not only surmounted the "stone wall" that the inclusion of Scouting into the Primary program represented at first, but she also brought honor to herself and co-workers in so doing. There would be other stone walls to hurdle, but her determination to go up to the first one and search for the "hidden ladder" made the other walls less formidable.

This woman, who so successfully met her first major challenge as president of an organization that was rapidly reaching world-wide dimensions, was born in Murray, Utah, on the first day of the twentieth century. She attended the University of Utah and taught school in the Murray (Utah) and Salt Lake City school districts. On June 28, 1923, she married Thomas Jennison Parmley, and traveled with him to Ithaca, New York, where he studied for his Ph.D. in physics at Cornell University. They returned to Salt Lake City in 1927 and reared their three children in the Bonneville Stake. In contrast to her predecessor, Adele Howells, who had spent years traveling around the world with her husband before her call to the Primary presidency, Sister Parmley traveled little before becoming Primary president but afterwards traveled more widely on Primary business than any other Primary president. On one occasion after her release, President Spencer W. Kimball asked her where she had traveled during her years as president. To his surprise, she replied, "President Kimball, I've been to every place where there is a mission [of the Church]. I've been to Japan, Taiwan ... Korea ... Singapore ... the Phillipines ... Okinawa ... Africa, South America, New Zealand, Australia, and in the thirty-four years I've been in, I have traveled and covered everywhere there has been a stake."[7]

When Sister Parmley joined the board in 1941, there were 147 stakes in the Church, all within the boundaries of the United States, Canada, and Hawaii. Board members were able to visit nearly every stake once a year, meeting stake and ward workers and discussing their problems. "At first," Sister Parmley remembered, "when you were working with the ward workers, you could get right down to the nitty gritties and work with them on how they would work with children.... You could get down to the functioning of the Primary." When meetings later included only stake leaders, she said, "you have to work more [on] leadership responsibilities and how they can then motivate the wards to do the work."[8] The annual conferences held in Salt Lake City for stake and mission representatives always brought at least one representative from nearly every stake or mission. But the Church was growing, not only within established stakes but also outward to new areas, and changes were inevitable.

In the first decade of Sister Parmley's administration the Primary nearly doubled in membership, growing from 157,223 members to more than 291,961. With this growth, the work of the general board correspondingly increased and more board members were needed. From thirty-six members when Sister Parmley took office, the board swelled to a high of seventy in 1970. More than thirty committees within the board worked to cover the wide range of programs in which the Primary was involved, including development of a new curriculum and the preparation of annual and ongoing programs, such as the sacrament meeting presentation, reverence program, Penny Parade promotion, summer program, April conference, regional meetings, Lamanite Primaries, home Primaries, Primaries for the handicapped, music, inservice, translation, Scouting, and all the age-groups. The presidency divided the responsibility for supervision of each of these areas, Sister Parmley always retaining supervision of the boys' program. A prescribed division of responsibility had never been systematically worked out for the members of the presidency before Sister Parmley's term of office. Assignments had been informally decided, usually based on interest or capability. These assignments were often rotated. Thus, in conventions and conferences all of the members of the presidency met together to discuss the program and problems. In 1963 Sister Parmley initiated a division of responsibilities that would align the duties of the general, stake, and ward presidents and those of each of the counselors. This arrangement greatly facilitated the use of leadership meetings and standardized the administration of the program all over the Church. Seven women served as counselors to Sister Parmley: Arta M. Hale, Florence H. Richards, Leone W. Doxey, Lucile C. Reading, Naomi W. Randall, Eileen R. Dunyon, and Florence R. Lane. They were all chosen from the board to serve as counselors.

While the general board was growing in number, membership

of stake boards decreased. After a pilot program proved to be successful, the general board announced in 1963 a reduction to a minimum of four the number of stake board members considered necessary to conduct the affairs of a stake Primary; later the minimum number was increased to eight. From a board of fifteen or sixteen in some stakes, this represented a substantial reduction. The plan was designed to allow the wards to retain more of their experienced workers.

The expansion of the Church in membership and area brought Sister Parmley up against another stone wall: adapting the Primary to meet the needs and circumstances of children and the women who worked with them all over the world. The problem she faced is exemplified in a simple change that was as obvious as it was necessary. A favorite song of the Trail Builders from the time it was commissioned by May Anderson in 1925 was the "Trail Builder Hymn," written by Theodore E. Curtis. But how could it be sung by the Trail Builders in Taiwan or Finland or New Zealand with words that said, "Oh, we are the boy Trail Builders, Out west where the sunsets glow...." And reasoning that all Mormon children were Zion's boys and girls, not just seven- and eight-year-olds, she found that class name inappropriate, too. Addressing herself to the problem with the same vigor with which she had tackled Scouting, Sister Parmley began to implement a series of changes in the age groups, which had not been appreciably altered since they were first established in their entirety by May Anderson in 1930.

The Zion's Boys and Girls gave way to Co-Pilots and Top-Pilots (later changed to Right Way and Choose-the-Right Pilots), names to which modern-day children could relate. The nameless Younger Groups, called Skylets in 1961, were given the individual class names of Sunbeams (four-year-olds), Stars (five-year-olds), and Rainbows (six-year-olds) between 1956 and 1958. Replacing the Home Builders in 1959 were the Lihomas, an acronym for Little Home Makers, comprising the Gaynotes, Firelights, and Merrihands. The boys' groups remained as they had been.

As these new individual class programs were developed to be applicable to all types of Primaries and all Primary children, it was no longer necessary to have special lessons for home and mission Primaries. All Primary children, as far as possible, were to utilize the same program, adapting only to meet specific needs.

Another aspect of the challenge that a worldwide church presented to Sister Parmley was maintaining contact with local workers. In 1962 individual auxiliary stake conventions and institutes were discontinued. In a correlated movement, representatives from all the general boards were assigned on a rotating basis to attend quarterly stake conferences with General Authorities, to conduct training meetings for ward and stake workers and to speak in the general sessions of the stake conference to explain and encourage participation in their programs. When the Church was divided into geographic regions, regional meetings became the contact point for general and local auxiliary officers. During 1973, the final year in which all regions were visited, board members attended 242 regional conventions. Eighty years before, board members had visited stakes at their invitation, and costs were covered by the nickels contributed by Primary children. In 1973 the general Primary presidency determined where the board would visit, and it took more than nickels to fly them to Primaries in the distant parts of the world! Clearly, annual visits to the regions, like the previous visits to the stakes, became impossible, and changes were again inevitable. In 1974 the auxiliaries were restricted to thirty regions of their choice, although the Primary—that year and in succeeding years—actually visited more because of special requests or pressing problems in some of the regions. At present, sixty regions are selected and visited. Originally two or more board members traveled together, but at present one representative from the board is assigned to a region along with a board member from another auxiliary.

With the annual regional conferences and the general Primary conference each April, stake Primary workers continued to have opportunity for two direct contacts annually with the general board. When the visits were curtailed, the board could still keep annual contact through its yearly general conferences.

But even the traditional Primary conference was destined to succumb to the requisites of an increasingly larger and more cosmopolitan Church. As stakes became established in more and more non-English speaking areas, interpreters were required in the department sessions to accommodate the Primary workers from these areas. But the challenge of communication with the multinational Primary workers was more than linguistic. With brand-new converts sitting alongside lifelong members in the conference sessions, Sister Parmley recognized that the meetings were not "touching the lives" of all workers and "giving the help that was needed.

A woman who had lived in Salt Lake City all her life, was well versed in the Church, and had been in Primary for years," she realized, "needed a different kind of help than this little sister that was just a new convert coming from South America or from Japan and had never worked in the Church."[9] Even while recognizing the difficulties the worldwide Church was presenting to established procedures such as Primary conference, Sister Parmley said, "I didn't have any idea that it would be done away with. I just thought it was part of the Church and was something that would last forever." But it did not. In April 1975, the Primary held its sixty-ninth and last general conference. In June of that year, the First Presidency instructed all the auxiliaries that only regional conferences would be held thereafter. Though at first surprised with the announcement, Sister Parmley recognized the inspired wisdom in the decision.

A request most universally made by stake workers in response to a questionnaire sent out by Sister Hinckley in 1940 was that there be more contact with the general board. Thirty years later the board could no longer accommodate such a request. "The growth of the Church," Sister Parmley lamented, "has made many more problems than we had."[10] The answer to this latest challenge at first seemed to be the same one that Sister Hinckley and

Sister Howells had found during the wartime restriction of visits: contact would have to be made by mail.

The Primary was already well entrenched in the process of writing and distributing publications to carry on its work. Besides periodic revisions of lesson manuals with accompanying handbooks, the board prepared special guides for ward and stake, branch and district Primaries; individual activity books for older Primary children; visual aid enrichment packets for teachers; instructions for mission, home, and summer primaries; special programs for ward conferences and summer Primary; numerous booklets on Scouting; guidelines and helps on teacher training, music, and the reverence program; and numerous play and activity bulletins. The "Stake Quarterly Bulletin" had been discontinued in 1947, but by 1956 it was necessary to reinstate a monthly written communication to field workers. The "Primary Script" replaced the stake bulletin, often containing as many as sixty pages of information, spiritual thoughts, and reprints of General Authorities' talks at Primary conference.

Unlike her predecessors, Sister Parmley had to meet the problem of communication with Primary workers other than with more printed material. Even while the need increased as personal contact decreased, the Primary board found itself moving out of the writing and publishing phase of its work. As the Church began to centralize the planning, writing, and distributing of educational materials for all auxiliaries, the Primary was left to carry on its program with only a minimal amount of published material. The Church was too large, the programs too numerous for any one organization to produce unlimited publications. Thus Sister Parmley faced the dual challenge of fewer visits along with fewer publications. Part of the solution to the problem was met in the standardization of lesson material. The key to meeting the rest of the challenge seemed to be in the effectiveness of the regional meetings for dispensing information even when general board members could not attend. Limited in 1973 to a single-page "Primary Dispatch" (from the once sixty-page "Primary Script"), the board now must present the entire year's program, detailing its implementation and anticipating questions, in the regional meeting packet of information that goes with the visiting board member or to Primary leaders in regions where board members are not assigned. The packet contains instructional materials, a filmstrip of visual aids, a tape recording of the Primary president's message, and other information necessary for administering Primary during the coming year. In the regions where general board members are assigned, they present the material. In the others, the Regional Representative currently selects a stake Primary leader to prepare and present the material. The future will bring other changes.

To keep at least minimal grass roots contact, beginning in 1962 Sister Parmley assigned board members to various stakes in or near the Salt Lake Valley with which to become personally involved by attending the Primary meetings and activities and becoming acquainted with stake and ward workers. With a board of seventy, a number of stakes could be visited and their needs and strengths ascertained. In this way, Primary leaders kept themselves from becoming too far removed from the actual functioning of the Primary, though their personal contact with Primary workers was decreasing.

Since the days of Eliza R. Snow's first tune book and hymnbook for Primary children, the Primary has always been interested in recommending good music for children. Through the years it has published several songbooks. During Sister Parmley's administration two new children's songbooks were issued. One, *The Children Sing,* published in 1951, was used jointly by the Junior Sunday School and the Primary. It underwent several reprintings, including some in foreign languages. In 1970 a new collection of songs, *Sing With Me,* was issued, again used conjointly by the Junior Sunday School and the Primary.

If the Primary had had a theme song in the nineteenth century it would likely have been "In Our Lovely Deseret," written by Eliza R. Snow and sung to a familiar marching tune. At a time when the Word of Wisdom was not yet thoroughly established as a Church practice, the song admonished children to "despise" tea and coffee and tobacco, to "drink no liquor" and eat very little meat, and to live a virtuous and faithful life:

In our lovely Deseret, Where the Saints of God have met,
There's a multitude of children all around;
They are generous and brave, They have precious souls to save,
They must listen, and obey the gospel's sound.

CHORUS:
Hark! hark! hark! 'tis children's music—
Children's voices, O how sweet,
When in innocence and love, Like the angels up above,
They with happy hearts and cheerful faces meet.

That the children may live long, and be beautiful and strong,
Tea and coffee and tobacco they despise,
Drink no liquor, and they eat but a very little meat;
They are seeking to be great and good and wise.

They should be instructed young How to watch and guard the tongue,
And their tempers train, and evil passion bind;
They should always be polite, And treat everybody right,
And in ev'ry place be affable and kind.

They must not forget to pray, night and morning, ev'ry day,
For the Lord to keep them safe from ev'ry ill,
And assist them to do right, that with all their mind and might,
They may love Him, and may learn to do His will.[11]

One Primary boy from Cache Valley, Utah, evidently heeded the words of the song. In a letter to the *Woman's Exponent* in 1881 he proudly announced that he was "a Mormon boy and never drank tea or coffee." Many generations of Mormon boys and girls may have gained their first understanding of the Word of Wisdom through the words of that song. Although Sister Snow wrote "In Our Lovely Deseret" in 1867 for the Sunday School, it was quickly adopted by the Primary, especially when she regularly requested it to be sung at Primary conferences that she visited throughout the territory. It was sung for other occasions, too. At the death of longtime Kaysville (Utah) Ward Primary president Jane Blood, in 1898, all of the Primary children of her ward lined the walk in front of her house, each holding a small bouquet of flowers. The children preceded the pallbearers in the procession to the cemetery, and after the burial they placed their bouquets on the grave, completely covering it. Then they sang "In Our Lovely Deseret," a favorite hymn that Sister Blood had taught them.[12]

For the current generation of Primary children all over the world, their theme song may well be "I Am a Child of God," written by Naomi W. Randall and Mildred T. Pettit. Sister Randall, a member of the Primary board, was asked by Sister Parmley to prepare a new song for the Primary Conference of April 1957. Sister Parmley suggested that she write the song in conjunction with Sister Pettit, a former board member then living in California, who had written several other Primary songs. Sister Randall wrote the words first and presented them to the general board on January 31, 1957. The minutes noted: "The words were lovely and truly touched the hearts of the members assembled." Then she sent them on to Sister Pettit, who in a week's time composed the music. "I Am a Child of God" is the musical heir to Eliza R. Snow's "O My Father" and in a child's words declares the same truths:

I am a child of God, And he has sent me here,
Has given me an earthly home With parents kind and dear.
CHORUS:
Lead me, guide me, walk beside me, Help me find the way.
Teach me all that I must do To live with him someday.

I am a child of God, And so my needs are great;
Help me to understand his words, Before it grows too late.

I am a child of God, Rich blessings are in store;
If I but learn to do his will, I'll live with him once more.

I am a child of God; His promises are sure.
Celestial glory shall be mine If I can but endure.[13]

The chorus of that well-loved song, sung not only by children but by their parents too, reinforces the long-held charge of Primary workers to lead, guide, and teach Primary children the principles of the gospel. Accepting the challenge of these words as a personal mandate, Sister Parmley infused the teacher training program with renewed vision and vigor. Taking over responsibility for writing its own teacher training lessons some years before, the Primary geared them all to the particular needs of women teaching children and the types of lessons they were assigned to teach. Primary leaders were sensitive to the strengths and weaknesses of their teachers. When overzealous teachers began inundating their lessons with attractive but overabundant visual aids, Sister Parmley decided to devote an entire Primary conference to the wise use of visual aids and then followed through on that particular aspect of teaching in the next year's teacher training manual. From this conference came the idea of visual aid packets to accompany the lesson manuals, thus standardizing the use of visual aids through the Primaries.

The educational premise for teaching children had not changed significantly from what it had been when Sister Felt and Sister Anderson had introduced the principles of progressive education into the Primary program. The teacher training manual for 1953, which introduced the term "inservice," issued a statement of this philosophy:

More and more we are coming to realize that childhood is the most important period in the life of the individual.... If we better understand the forces that contribute to human growth and development we can contribute to the welfare of children.

To accomplish our purpose we have attempted to bring together in this book some of the current findings and viewpoints in the rapidly advancing field of understanding the child. So our essential reason for studying about child development is that we might know better how to make the

Gospel of Jesus Christ function in the lives of children.[14]

The value of understanding the needs of the child, recognizing the varying age characteristics, and responding to the individual variations continued to underlie the approach to teaching that the Primary would utilize for the next seventeen years. But an understanding of child development was not the only principle of good teaching to which the Primary addressed itself. The conscientious teacher was advised to prepare herself not only by learning to understand the children she taught, but also by studying the scriptures and living gospel principles, as well as mastering standard teaching skills and procedures.

One board member visiting a stake in Dallas, Texas, met with six bishops and found that none had been members of the Church longer than two years. She then visited a class of Primary children and heard the young, newly converted teacher say: "See this flower in this picture? Heavenly Father is in this flower. See the sky? He is in the sky and the clouds. He is also in your own heart." The board member concluded that there were many new convert teachers who had not fully lost old dogma in learning the gospel, and so the decision was made to prepare a manual for teachers, *This Is the Truth,* dealing exclusively with the principles and ordinances of the gospel.[15] It was designed to "give teachers a feeling for and an understanding of the lessons" they taught in Primary.

In 1960 the Primary published one of its first teaching source books, *Three Steps to Good Teaching,* a compilation of basic teaching principles for Primary teachers. This was followed in 1968 by a small pamphlet, *The HOW Book,* which was aimed toward the inexperienced teacher and covered such teaching problems as how to use the chalkboard, how to ask questions, how to get and keep attention, how to use music, and how to tell stories.

In 1970, when the correlation process drew teacher training into a Church-sponsored program, the Primary joined the other auxiliaries in presenting a teacher development program consisting of six yearly series of lessons. The Primary taught the lessons within its own inservice program. At the completion of the six-year course, lessons were repeated from the last two series until 1978, when the Primary once again planned its own inservice lessons. Based on material in the newly revised and expanded *HOW Book for Teaching Children,* the lessons also made use of a resource book, *Teaching—No Greater Call,* developed by the Church Teacher Development Committee in 1978. This series of lessons, however, was merely an interim program. Following a growing trend toward more local development of programs, the inservice lessons of the future for the Primary will be designed to help local leaders assess the needs of their teachers and to utilize the *HOW Book for Teaching Children* and the new resource book to meet those needs. Once again, as in early days, the initiative to develop at least this aspect of the curriculum has been placed in the hands of stake and ward leaders.

The correlation of the teacher training program in 1970 was but one step in a process that presented Sister Parmley with another of her many challenges as Primary president. At general conference in 1961, a new Church coordinating council was introduced, whose purpose was to correlate Church curriculum, activities, and programs as they were implemented through the priesthood, the auxiliaries, and the home. The goal of the committee, as explained by Elder Harold B. Lee in 1967, was "to place the priesthood in the place where the Lord had placed it: to watch over the Church," with all Church programs to come under the direct authority and direction of the priesthood.

While the theory of correlation was recognized as mandatory for the efficient development and implementation of Church programs, particularly in a worldwide setting, it marked a tremendous change in the functioning of the individual auxiliaries. After eighty-three years, the Primary now looked to a central curriculum committee to develop the concepts and write the lessons for Primary children. Representatives from both the Sunday School and the Primary general boards would serve on this committee, but responsibility for developing their own lesson plans no longer rested with the individual auxiliaries. Thus by 1970 two basic features of the Primary, lesson writing and teacher training, were being developed and coordinated by general Church committees, and the distribution of the materials was handled by a general Church distribution center. Thirty years of Primary leadership in which total responsibility for the organization had been vested in the presidency did not drop easily from the shoulders of Sister Parmley: "When you work through the Correlation Committee you go through the curriculum department.... You go through editing. You go through publications. You go through printing, publishing, distribution, and you work with so many people. It's quite different than when you had the complete responsibility of it.... When you had questions you'd...go only to your two advisors."[16]

After shepherding the Primary Association through the difficult years in which the new correlation process was taking its first steps, Sister Parmley was convinced of its necessity. "I think the correlation program was inspired by President Lee," she said. "I think it was a hard adjustment, but I agree that it's the right thing. And if things aren't right after going through all those committees then something's wrong.... Now that it goes through all these different phases I think if someone doesn't find something wrong then we can be assured the material is good."[17] Sister Parmley met this latest stone wall in a spirit of cooperation and merged the goals and programs of the Primary into a larger Church-sponsored program for children without compromising the Primary's responsibility for its more than four hundred thousand members.

Explaining the value of a correlated program to workers at the Primary Conference in 1970, Elder Boyd K. Packer told them that "no organization needs stand alone; nor, indeed, can it fulfill its purpose if it were to do so. The strength of all organizations can sustain and help each organization. Then the power of the whole Church—indeed, the power of the priesthood—can be marshaled in defense of our children against the enticings of the evil one."

But more changes were destined to alter once again the function of the Primary after Sister Parmley's release in October 1974 and the subsequent call of Naomi M. Shumway. In 1977 the responsibility for planning lesson concepts was returned to the Primary, and a curriculum planning committee comprised only of Primary board members now develops lesson plans for every age group in the Primary. While the Sunday School and Primary were both teaching lessons based on the Articles of Faith under the correlation program, the Primary is planning new curriculum that will give it exclusive responsibility to teach the gospel principles as contained in the Articles of Faith and supported by scriptures primarily from the Book of Mormon, returning to the subject matter determined by Primary leaders and their advisers nearly half a century ago. An innovation, however, is that the Articles of Faith are no longer reserved as lesson material for older Primary children. The four-year-olds will begin their Primary experience by learning about the First Article of Faith. This change is a result of current findings by child psychologists and educators suggesting that children grasp basic concepts and retain them at a much younger age than was once thought.

With lesson planning once again its own responsibility, the Primary has resumed its place in what has come to be a cyclical pattern of alternating independent and shared responsibility for its programs and curriculum. Since 1907 the Primary has willingly conformed to the directives of the oft-revived correlation movements, providing leisure-time activity for children when gospel training was given to the religion classes, and teaching gospel lessons when the religion classes were discontinued. It has adapted to Church-sponsored teacher training programs or initiated its own when Church programs were completed. It has shared lesson planning and writing with respected Church educators and assigned curriculum writers but has eagerly developed its own lessons when given responsibility to do so.

Japanese Primary children at annual Primary festival, August 1977

Chapter Nine

"A Difference Almost Miraculous"

In 1884, three years after being appointed Cache Valley (Utah) Stake Primary president, Jane Hyde Molen visited the small branch of the Church at Washakie, an Indian village near the Malad Valley in Idaho. She was delighted with the Primary that functioned in that branch and reported to the *Woman's Exponent* that the "good order of their meetings might well be a pattern to a more enlightened race."[1]

The Washakie Branch Primary may have been a model of reverence in 1884, but many current Primary workers have probably felt more like the Goshen, Utah, Primary counselor who told the children in 1879 that "she thought they might try to be orderly for the one hour and that these Societies were for their especial benefit and they should pay attention."[2] Discipline in Primary has always been a challenge to leaders. The grading of classes in 1895 relieved some of the obstacles to order, and over the years new programs have been introduced to capture and retain the interest and attention of the children.

In 1941 May Hinckley initiated a project for teachers for "being orderly in Church," with a slogan, "I will not talk in Church," incorporated into the Primary Teachers' Creed. Later, these yearly projects were expanded to include the children, and a new statement of behavioral commitment to some aspect of reverence was introduced each year. Soon after Sister Parmley took office, the yearly project was changed to "Our Standard," continuing the strong emphasis placed on developing reverent concepts and behavior. Approval of this effort was noted when the behavioral problems committee of the Primary board reported that "the brethren were very pleased that the behavior problem is being given such detailed consideration."[3] In 1955 the board decided to launch an all-out effort to achieve reverence in Primary by a uniform appeal and message to be presented in each departmental session of the Primary Conference in April. The theme was "A Disciplined Child in Primary."[4]

In 1967, Sister Parmley implemented a reverence program that has been a prominent feature of the Primary ever since. During the opening exercises of each Primary meeting the officiating officer gives a three-minute reverence presentation with appropriate stories and songs. Sometimes children take part in a brief dialogue about reverent behavior. Each year a new theme is chosen and some phase of the theme is incorporated into the weekly presentations. For example, in 1971-72 Primary children all over the world were reciting "I want to be reverent" each week after hearing a story reminding them that their parents wanted them to be reverent, that their Father in Heaven expected them to be reverent, or that reverence is a special feeling.

The emphasis on reverent behavior, which became an identifiable part of the Primary program during Sister Parmley's administration, had received impetus from President Howells too. In his address at the 1948 Primary Conference, Elder Harold B. Lee spoke of his concern for the lack of reverent behavior in houses of worship, and also about inappropriate music, stories, and pictures that did not invoke a spirit of reverence. He advised against adding fictitious incidents or descriptions when telling or dramatizing the lives of sacred characters. He then asked the women assembled: "What can Primary do about it?" Accepting his challenge, Sister Howells and her board urged Primary leaders to stress in their teaching not only reverent behavior, but a reverent attitude toward sacred things as well. As one step toward developing reverence in Primary meetings, they analyzed the music recommended and made the suggestions, reemphasized later by Sister Parmley's board, that the familiar "Primary Penny Song," which had ushered children in or out of Primary for many years—perhaps a little too enthusiastically—be replaced by another song that would not distract from a reverential attitude. The children with birthday pennies were to be honored by sitting on the stand during opening exercises. A "Happy Birthday" song would then be sung to them when they deposited their pennies in an appropriate container.[5] Attempting to meet two needs, a "need for reverence and a need to recognize children who brought their birthday pennies," Sister Parmley also found the Penny march a disturbing feature, and, like Sister Howells, she felt that children should be more personally recognized during their birthday week and honored individually for their contribution to the hospital. Other activity songs that required overly active participation were replaced by quiet rest songs that provided physical respite without disrupting a reverent atmosphere.

Another means of developing reverence was the introduction of the pre-Primary. Teachers with preschool children were often obliged to bring them to prayer meeting, held for twenty minutes prior to Primary. In order to keep them orderly, the board suggested that one teacher or officer meet with these children for singing, storytelling, or an activity to keep them occupied. Some stakes worked out booklets with ideas for teachers of the pre-Primary, and others enlisted the help of junior and senior high school girls. While the general board endorses the idea of a pre-Primary, its organization and functioning are left to the determination of the individual wards and stakes.

The success of the reverence program was attested to by Primary adviser Gordon B. Hinckley, who told Primary presidencies in 1967:

I am confident that because of your effort we are coming to have increased reverence in our church buildings. The simple song of reverence, the quiet example of officers and teachers, the orderly planning of meetings have slowly but wondrously borne good fruit. It was not perceptible as it happened, but as I have looked across fifty years from the time I first at-

159

tended Primary until now, I note a difference almost miraculous. You have seen the need and accomplished a remarkable thing...."[6]

Other differences "almost miraculous" occurred in Primary during Sister Parmley's administration. One was a program to bring Primary to every Mormon child regardless of his physical or mental capacity. Nearly eighty years after Aurelia Rogers expressed concern for the spiritual welfare of young Mormon boys, two other mothers voiced a similar concern for their boys. But there was a difference. Their sons were mentally retarded. Gordon and Barry attended the Fairmont Park Training Center in Salt Lake City, where they enjoyed the association of other children like themselves and the help and encouragement of sympathetic persons other than family members on weekdays. But Sundays were long and uneventful. These children did not fit into any Church program. Their spiritual development depended on home instruction, which busy parents could not always provide on a regular basis. The repeated efforts of these two mothers to establish a Sunday School for the handicapped under general Church auspices were not successful because of the logistical demands such a program would entail at that time.

Undaunted, they decided to present their problem directly to the Primary. A phone call to Sister Parmley resulted in an assignment to board member Ada S. Van Dam to determine the possibility of creating a special Primary for the children attending the Fairmont Park School. In attendance were the Utah State supervisor of Day Care Centers for the Handicapped, the president of the Salt Lake County Association for Retarded Children, which sponsored the Fairmont Park School, a teacher at the school, the Granite Stake Primary presidency, who would direct the Primary, and four mothers of children attending the school, including the two who initiated the project. The date was November 20, 1960, and in ten days the first Primary for the Handicapped opened at three P.M. in the Forest Dale Ward chapel, for thirty-five children.[7]

This was the beginning of a program for the handicapped that would develop within the next eighteen years into a Churchwide concern. In the meantime, the Primary developed its own guidelines and lessons for teachers of mentally handicapped children. The Star manual was used for lessons, and graduation requirements were determined on an individual basis. Music was discovered to be an excellent medium for teaching gospel concepts because the children were able to memorize words set to music more easily than those that were not. One group of children, having difficulty in memorizing the Articles of Faith, quickly learned them when their talented music leader set them to music. Hundreds of children have graduated from Primary and enjoyed the benefits of its program through these special Primaries.

The Forest Dale Ward Primary served as a pilot project. It was funded by the Granite Stake and the families of the children involved, and teachers were recruited from among stake members and the mothers of the children. With the help of many people, the Primary was an immediate success and prompted the organization of other units in nearby areas. The South Davis Stake, north of Salt Lake City, organized a Primary for the handicapped the next year with sixteen children grouped into three classes and staffed by ten officers and teachers. The Kearns, Granger, and Wilford Stakes followed in 1962 with Primaries ranging in membership from ten to nineteen children. A large Primary for nearly eighty-four mentally retarded children was organized in 1964 in the Lorin Farr Stake in Ogden. In the following years additional Primaries were organized throughout Utah and in several other states. Primaries for the handicapped had become an integral part of the Primary program.

With the organization of the National Association for Retarded Children in 1950, an awareness of the needs of mentally handicapped children on a national level spurred the passage of a number of subsequent government programs providing for the development of research, teacher training, and education of the mentally retarded. Other legislation provided for the handicapped in the schools and special centers within the states. These separate

161

programs culminated in 1975 in the passage of Public Law 94-142, the Education for All Handicapped Children Act, which acknowledged the right of a free and appropriate education in the least restrictive environment for all handicapped children. Studies had shown that educable handicapped children achieved in integrated situations as well as or better than they did in segregated groups.

This program of mainstreaming handicapped children into normal social and educational environments has influenced the policy of the Primary. Wherever possible, the mentally handicapped child is now assimilated into an appropriate Primary class based on his mental and social development levels, and Primaries for the handicapped operate only for those children who cannot be thus assimilated.

Primaries for the handicapped are organized on three levels:

1. The individual class attached to a ward Primary.

2. The separate Primary within a stake, supervised and staffed by stake personnel.

3. The separate Primary within a region or multiregion supervised by an assigned stake under the direction of regional priesthood authority.

Blind and deaf children, along with other physically handicapped children, are also brought into the regular Primary program wherever possible. Although a special Primary was initiated in Ogden at the Utah School for the Blind and Deaf in 1952, the policy of mainstreaming these children has taken hold. In many instances the assimilation of blind children is easier than that of deaf children in that the child can hear the lessons, learn the songs, and participate in many handiwork projects. The Church has also produced some children's reading material in Braille.

The deaf child presents a different kind of problem. Visual materials can be captioned, but the presentation of lessons by the untrained teacher is often difficult. While the Church has a number of branches for the deaf, often the children of deaf parents are not deaf themselves and do not need special instruction. Conversely, few deaf children have deaf parents, and transporting these children to the special branches is often difficult or even impossible.

Available to teachers of deaf children and for the use of the children themselves are several Church-produced aids: *A Dictionary of Sign Language Terms* for unique Church terminology, captioned videotapes of the Book of Mormon and Church history, and heavily illustrated Book of Mormon stories for beginning readers with glossaries of terms, people, and places. Teachers near universities are encouraged whenever possible to learn from these institutions methods of teaching the deaf.

In 1976, the special curriculum division of the Church's Instructional Development Department published *Teaching the Handicapped: A Self-Instruction In-Service Packet,* consisting of a workbook and two cassettes, recommended for those teachers in any program of the Church who are teaching the handicapped. One vital lesson in the manual deals with teaching normal children and adults to understand and integrate the handicapped, essential to the mainstreaming program.

Acting on the concern of two loving mothers for the spiritual well-being of their disabled sons, Primary women once again proved to be pioneers in answering the needs of Latter-day Saint children. And the measurable spiritual development of these special children, attested to by both the children and their parents, has been the happy result. One little Primary boy, whose life is marked by different time guides than other children, expressed his joy in the new experience that Primary had brought to him by daily asking his mother, "How many more sleeps until Primary day?" Teachers have found themselves swept into a compelling commitment to the program almost in spite of themselves. One told Sister Van Dam, "If ever I make mistakes or do anything wrong, please help me and correct me and give me suggestions—but please, oh please, don't ever take this Primary away from me."[8]

Primary has made a difference in the lives of non-Mormon children too. Two young women missionaries serving in the mission field about the same time that Sister Parmley became

Primary president quickly learned, as many had done before them, that Primary was a valuable missionary tool. Discouraged after months of fruitless tracting in Wheaton, a subdivision of Silver Springs, Maryland, they wondered what to do next. Spring answered their question. The warm weather brought hundreds of children out-of-doors and the young women decided to organize a Primary. The first problem was finding a place to meet. As they continued knocking on doors, they met a woman who expressed no interest in the gospel but a strong interest in the Primary. Though she had no children of her own, she offered the unfinished basement in her home for the meetings. Indulging in a bit of wishful thinking, the missionaries thought how nice it would be to have a rug to cover the cement floor and went so far as to dream of acquiring a piano. How surprised they were to learn that a woman who was moving from the neighborhood was leaving behind a blue rug and an old piano. With the basement room, the blue rug, and the old piano, the missionaries began their Primary. Week after week the room filled up with children, and doors opened to the missionaries when they were identified as the teachers of the "Mormon Bible School." Within just a few years that little neighborhood Primary had brought enough members into the Church that plans were made to break ground for a chapel.[9]

Primaries outside the United States have not always fared so well. A report from Sister Parmley after a visit to Europe in 1961 indicated some of the problems faced by many mission Primaries. "I sat down with a [Primary] stake presidency in England," she reported after one visit, "and found none of them had a telephone and they lived in different cities quite a few miles apart and they didn't have money to travel. I thought then, 'What would the Primary presidency in Salt Lake do if they didn't have telephones?'"[10] Besides communication and travel problems, Sister Parmley found that many new converts were not accustomed to weekday religious meetings and did not or could not allow time for such meetings in their schedules. Lack of appropriate or adequate buildings for weekday services prevented the holding of

Primary in many areas. The financial responsibility for maintaining a ward or stake after conversion from a branch was new and heavy for inexperienced leaders, and auxiliaries were often underfunded. Though guides, handbooks, and lesson and song manuals were prepared for the missions, many small Primaries did not have sufficient funds to obtain them.

Withal, under the direction of determined leaders and concerned priesthood officers, Primary has been instituted wherever children of Primary age can gather, usually beginning as home Primaries. In Argentina, for example, a home Primary of twelve children proved to be quite successful. Three of the children belonged to the Latter-day Saint mother who conducted the Primary. The other nine were "not yet" members, as this confident and dedicated mother/Primary teacher characterized them. In Jerusalem a home Primary was organized by a mother for her children so that she and her husband could utilize the assistance of the Primary program in teaching them the principles of the gospel while living away from the Church. "Our oldest son," she wrote, "is preparing for his graduation from Primary this year, and will be the first to graduate from the Primary in Israel." One newly converted couple and their four children, living in General Santos City in the Philippine Islands, conducted a home Primary for their four children, but because of their inexperience in the Church, they asked the missionaries to assist. Within a short time, the Primary had grown to twenty and the missionaries had converted the parents of several of the children.

The home and neighborhood Primary program has always depended on the dedication and perseverance of a mother in the home who is willing to carry out a consistent program each week with her children and others who meet with them. More than a thousand home Primaries are functioning throughout the Church at the present time.

All aspects of the Primary program, including reverence, were supported and enriched by the *Children's Friend.* Envisioned by its founder as one day becoming solely a children's magazine, the

Children's Friend finally met that goal during Sister Parmley's administration. The process was slow but steady. By June 1954 the last of the mission lessons appeared in the magazine, since these were to be presented in a separate manual. Within two more years only two or three pages were allotted to messages for parents and teachers. One new feature introduced under Sister Parmley's direction appeared in connection with the Primary's new Primary/home partnership program, and was entitled the "Family Hour." The purpose of this series, according to its introduction in the July 1954 issue, was "to help bring about a close family relationship... by bringing members together as a family group and discussing problems, sharing ideas, hearing stories, and participating together in wholesome activities.[11] In each issue thereafter, the "Family Hour" presented ideas and lessons for family sharing, anticipating the Church's family home evening program, which superseded the "Family Hour" in 1961. The Primary/home partnership program was designed to bring parents into closer contact with the objectives of each age group by providing packets for parents with questions and suggested activities appropriate to the lessons they could share with their children. The close involvement of parents with their children through this program was appreciated by many parents. "We liked it," many of them told Sister Parmley, "when we knew what the children were being taught in Primary and then we could spend our time talking about it."[12]

The year 1961 brought a new face and format to the *Children's Friend*. At long last it truly appeared to be what its original founders had hoped it would be—a children's magazine. Only occasional brief articles for parents or teachers appeared during the next decade. Moreover, the magazine took on a bright, colorful, modern look, beginning with boldly colored wrap-around covers and continuing through colorful pages filled with bright illustrative material and vividly colored prints. Readers had been used to seeing soft-toned photographs of sweet-faced children or attractive drawings in one or two pleasant colors gracing the cover of the magazine, with few or no colored pictures within. But the January

1961 issue burst onto the children's scene with a splash that delighted most, even while dismaying a few. The new, abstract artwork was a radical departure from the comfortably familiar look associated with the magazine. The reaction was immediate and definite: "If this is a sample of all future issues you can cancel our subscription," said one reader. "Please don't let *The Children's Friend* be just another copy-cat of so-called modern art," wrote another.

Some readers did not like what had happened to Barnabee Bumbleberry, a series of boxed pictures and captions originated in 1953 by Naomi Randall and Phyllis Thorpe. Barnabee was originally drawn as a cherubic little boy with a tail-wagging terrier who had a series of adventures—or misadventures—that appealed to readers of all ages. In the hands of the new art, Barnabee became an abstract caricature with an elongated figure of a dog drawn in black ink against bright colored backgrounds. "Not even Barnabee escaped the horror of the new art," one reader wrote. "My children feel they have truly lost a good friend." The general board was itself divided over the effect of the magazine. One member, an artist, explained to the board the principles underlying modern art and suggested that "it is good art and a natural expression of the speed, motion and feeling of our times." Others reminded the group that criticism had continually been leveled against the previous art content of the magazine.

A more searching issue seemed to rest on the perception readers and board members had of what the magazine was to be. "Is the purpose of the magazine to become just another coloring book for the child's entertainment," asked one reader, "or is the magazine to instruct the child in the gospel of Jesus Christ?" Board members expressed the same concern. They did not want the *Children's Friend* to be just another child's magazine. They questioned the compatibility of the principles of the gospel with the principles of contemporary art, and questioned the new art as an appropriate medium for a Church magazine.[13]

The editorial board with the help of the priesthood advisers settled the matter by defining the purpose of the magazine as being a tool for teaching the gospel of Jesus Christ to boys and girls, which was somehow compromised by the dominating presence of the new art. The new look continued for the first six issues of 1961 and then gave way to a modified interpretation of modern art design. After the flurry of excitement subsided, the magazine eased through the transition from its longtime traditional appearance to a new but conservative contemporary art style without further problems. However modified, the magazine sported a new look designed to please the audience it was now addressing almost exclusively, the children.

In 1971, as part of the consolidation movement of the Church, the *Children's Friend* was placed with all other Church publications under the direction of the Church Publications Committee. Lucile C. Reading was called from her position as a counselor in the Primary general presidency to become editor of the new children's magazine, called *The Friend.* The magazine was no longer a direct responsibility of the Primary. It became the official Church magazine for children.

Under the wing of the Primary, the *Children's Friend* was much honored. Besides winning an award from the National Offset-Lithography Competition in 1953 for the Book of Mormon paintings, it won a second award in that competition in 1954. It also received three awards from the National Safety Council for "exceptional service to safety." It won awards from the National Association of Press Women, the Simpson Gallery of Fine Painting and Lithography, and the Mead Paper Company for outstanding printing.[14]

Although each Primary general president has also borne the title of editor of the *Children's Friend,* others have served in an advisory and managing capacity. No one served longer or more devotedly than Mary Jack, who joined the *Children's Friend* office staff as a typist in 1913, and who worked in various capacities, primarily as managing editor, until her retirement in 1970. Serving the magazine for all but eleven of its sixty-nine-year history, she saw it pass through its many transitions from teacher's handbook to children's leisure-time friend. Gladys D. Daines also gave years of valuable editorial service, specializing in art and layouts that served to complement the stories, poems, and articles that made up each issue. The *Children's Friend*—now the *Friend*—has been and continues to be a delightful companion to LDS and non-LDS children.

Of all the miraculous differences that Primary has made in the lives of children, perhaps none have been as dramatic as those which occurred through the Primary Children's Hospital. As counselor in the Primary presidency, Sister Parmley had assisted Adele Howells in overseeing the building of the new hospital. Only months before its completion, Sister Howells died and Sister Parmley had responsibility for opening the hospital and moving the children from the old convalescent home to the new facility.

On February 12, 1952, a stormy winter holiday, Sister Parmley and some of her board members and their husbands transferred the thirty-two excited young patients to their spacious new home. The medications and food supplies had been moved the previous day, and so, in spite of the storm, the children had to be moved. Ambulances, buses, and station wagons were called into service to transport the children as comfortably and safely as possible. With the blinding snow swirling all about, the caravan of vehicles inched its way from North Temple Street up the steep hill to the north bench of Salt Lake City, where the new hospital awaited its tenants. "I was really concerned with the great responsibility that day," Sister Parmley remembered, "but I'm sure the Lord blessed us because we were able to move all the children without any trouble."[15]

The children were ecstatic over their new accommodations. "There was a look of awe and wonder on their faces," Sister Parmley recalled, as she saw them look around at the beautiful rooms and then view the Salt Lake Valley lying below them. The little handful of children was almost lost in the spaciousness of the new structure and Sister Parmley actually wondered if the hospital would ever be filled. In a period of forty years, the Primary Children's Hospital had grown from a small ward of three or four beds, to a large but inadequate convalescent home accommodating twenty-five children, to a modern new sixty-bed facility with a large, well-equipped therapy room, an out-patient clinic, a children's library, two schoolrooms, a children's dining room where ambulatory patients could sit at little tables, and a dental department.

From 1913 to 1922, 72 children had been treated at the Groves' LDS Hospital through the Primary sponsorship program. In the first eight months of the convalescent home, 53 children received care, and 187 had been treated by the end of the second year of operation. In all, 5,907 children received care at the old children's hospital. Now the new hospital was completed.

In his address at the dedicatory service on March 2, 1952, President David O. McKay said: "The Primary Children's Hospital is a blessing to thousands of children in need of medical skill and careful nursing. It is a monument to all who believe in doing generous deeds to their fellowmen, meriting the approval of the Savior who said, 'These deeds shall thy memorial be. Fear not, thou didst them unto me.'"[16]

Sister Parmley's first thought at seeing the completed structure was "How will we use all that room!"[17] But within a decade it was necessary to add a new wing to the hospital to accommodate the growing services required by the numbers of children it served. The cost estimate for the new wing was a million dollars, and the Primary was asked to raise half of the amount. Sister Parmley invited the 75,000 Primary workers each to contribute one dollar, which they were to earn especially for the fund. The methods of earning money were widely varied and effective. Some women reported they had gathered pine nuts and sold them. Some picked and sold apples. Others gave piano lessons, haircuts, and luncheons. Some women baked pumpkin pies and sold them at Thanksgiving time. One woman sold rides on a donkey while another trimmed poodle dogs. One young Primary teacher with two babies still in diapers and on bottles reported that she was so tired each night that she was unable to do any extra work, so she just paid herself a dollar to sit down and rest. "I feel I've really earned it," she said. Instead of $75,000, the workers amassed $103,000.[18]

The hospital employees also participated in the fund raising, collecting $10,000. Hospital volunteers contributed $6,000. The doctors associated with the hospital sponsored a benefit ball which netted $28,000. The *Deseret News* with the Primary Association sponsored a premiere showing of the movie *Mary Poppins,* which added another $31,000 to the fund. Other individuals and business and social groups also made contributions. The new wing was completed and dedicated in June 1966.

This addition was but the first of many improvements made in order to provide a wide range of services. Ultimately the hospital would have its own pediatric surgeons, an emergency room, a birth defects center, and an enlarged department for outpatients. An inpatient psychiatric unit, to supplement the day-care center for emotionally disturbed children, and a ward for teenagers were later additions to the hospital.

The age limit for patients had been fourteen, but it was raised to eighteen when the LDS Hospital became overcrowded and the Primary Hospital had extra beds. Under the Primary's supervision, the teenage floor was managed differently than the other wards. It had a recreation room with a pool table, a record player, and games, and the ambulatory patients were permitted to visit the kitchen once a week to make cakes and other treats for their own parties. Both hot and cold food service was available on their floor, and those who were able could select their own food. At one time, when the teenage patients wanted some new records, they made cakes in the kitchen and sold them to visitors. From this project they were able to buy all the records they wanted. At Christmastime they decorated their floor, an activity that helped enliven their hospital stay.

Until 1975 the hospital was aided by the Primary Penny Parade, which in its last year of direct association with the hospital brought in over a million and a quarter dollars. Civic groups as well as individuals have made generous contributions through the years. Salt Lake City merchants have regularly brought surplus toys to the hospital shortly before Christmas, and other groups have also contributed toys and supplies. Sometimes homes and real property have been donated to the hospital through the wishes of individuals who have died without heirs. The income from their rental or sale, as stipulated in the wills of the donors, reverts to the hospital. In recent years a Women's Endowment Committee has sponsored an annual Festival of Trees. The beautifully decorated Christmas trees, donated by individuals or groups, are sold and the proceeds, often amounting to more than $100,000, are given to the hospital.

The hospital was originally supervised by a Board of Trustees with the general president of the Primary as chairman. In 1939, however, when May Anderson was released as Primary president, she was asked to retain her position as president of the hospital board. She remained as president until Adele Cannon Howells was given that responsibility in 1943 when she became general Primary president. In 1945 Frances Grant Bennett was called as vice-president of the board of trustees with the specific assignment to assist in the supervision of the building of the new hospital. Although the hospital as a social service unit was under the direction of the Presiding Bishop's office, no member of that body ever sat with the board until 1970, when Robert L. Simpson, counselor to the Presiding Bishop, was asked to be chairman of the board. Sister Parmley, the last Primary president to serve as chairman, became vice-president. That same year, when the Health Services Corporation board of trustees was organized to oversee all LDS hospitals, Sister Parmley was released from the hospital board and appointed to the new HSC board. Two Primary board members, Myrl W. Hamilton and Margaret P. Ottosen, then represented the Primary on the Primary hospital governing board, which functioned under the direction of the HSC board. Because of the expanding services offered by the hospital, the name was changed in 1973 to the Primary Children's Medical Center. The following year, as part of a move to divest itself of all of its hospitals, the Church relinquished control of the Primary Children's Medical Center to a private Health Services Corporation.

From its beginning the Primary Children's Hospital has been open to children of all races and creeds. No child has been turned away if the hospital could help his condition. Usually the child is recommended by his parents or a physician who provides a diagnosis of the case for the information of the hospital staff. An emergency case does not require a prior diagnosis. A social worker meets with the family after the patient arrives at the hospital to determine the financial responsibility of the family. Whenever parents are able to pay, even in part, they are asked to do so. Otherwise the children become Primary service patients, and the hospital assumes the costs of treatment, utilizing funds collected in fund-raising campaigns.

One serious emergency in 1966 involved a small boy from Chile with a serious heart problem whose mother brought him to Salt Lake City without prior communication because she feared he would not live through the time necessary to make proper arrangements. The doctors provided temporary treatment in order to strengthen him for open heart surgery. The success of the surgery could not be determined for four or five days, but on the last day of waiting it was discovered that the child had a bleeding ulcer that would need immediate surgery. A second operation after open heart surgery was full of risks, but the doctors felt there was no hope for the boy without it. Members of the Primary general board united their faith and prayers and fasted in behalf of the boy. The operation was a success, and in time the boy was completely healed. His mother took him home well and happy. So well, in fact, that his Primary teacher later complained in a letter to the hospital, "You did too good a job on this little boy. He's the most active boy. We can't control him now in Primary or meetings." In 1978, the boy, Angel Necochea, was serving a full-time mission in the Chile Osorno Mission.

Another patient was a child whose bones broke at the slightest pressure, a rare malady; he had been abandoned by the side of a road by his parents in Bolivia. He was taken to a crippled children's home but received no medical treatment. The supervisor of the home contacted the Primary Children's Hospital, offering to pay transportation costs for him. The hospital agreed to accept him. The boy, whose limbs were badly deformed from many untreated fractures, underwent many operations until all of his bones were straightened and reinforced with pins. When his treatment was over, he had no one to return to at home, so one of the interns at the hospital adopted him and took him to live with his family in Idaho.

Leasinia, another patient, came from Tonga on a foggy night in December 1962, with a tag around her neck that read: "I don't need money but I am looking for the Primary Children's Hospital. Help me find the hospital." Because of a defect in her spine, Leasinia was unable to use any of her limbs. After a critical but successful operation, she remained a year at the hospital for convalescence. When she returned home, she was walking, but she had gained more than the use of her limbs. She had learned English and attended school for the first time in her life, and she had made many friends from all over the United States, Mexico, Canada, and from the Pacific Islands. When Sister Parmley visited the Primary in Tonga sometime later, she saw Leasinia dancing in an MIA dance festival.

Koki, a Tahitian boy, was unable to walk when he arrived at the hospital. Two years and eight operations later, the use of his legs had been restored, and he was able to return home. Ten years later, when Sister Parmley was visiting a stake conference in Hawaii, the stake president said, "We have a surprise for you. Will Koki stand up?" In the middle of the audience a fine young man stood up. Afterwards Sister Parmley learned that Koki had served a mission, was presently attending the Church College in Hawaii, and was to be married in a few weeks. In addition, he was dancing every night as a performer in the Polynesian Cultural Center. His words to Sister Parmley were, "What would my life have been if it hadn't been for the hospital?" After leaving Hawaii, Sister Parmley went to Tahiti to meet the Primary president there. What a delightful surprise it was to discover she was Koki's mother!

The hospital has treated patients from as many as twenty-six states and thirteen foreign countries in a single year. Doctors from all over the country, acquainted with the services provided by the hospital, recommend special cases to its care.

Because so many children in the early years of the hospital spend many recuperative months there, Primary is conducted regularly under the direction of the Ensign Stake. Children of all denominations are invited to attend. The parents of some of these non-LDS children have discovered the Church through the illnesses of their children. One non-LDS family brought their critically ill infant to the hospital on the recommendation of their physician, who told them that their own church-sponsored hospital was unable to provide the necessary treatment. Unfortunately, their child could not be saved, and the hospital personnel were concerned that the parents would regret their not having taken the child to their own hospital where it could have received religious rites prior to its death. Some days later, however, the parents returned to the Primary Hospital and remarked about the spirit they had felt during those anxious hours. They wanted to learn more about the Church. A short time later they were converted and were instrumental in the conversion of some of their friends.

When the Primary surrendered the hospital in 1974, it little resembled its small beginnings. By 1974 it was a large medical center with a psychiatric department providing outpatient service for 250 children between the ages of six and eighteen every week. The day-care center served thirty children five days a week. A residential treatment home accommodated eight children. An inpatient psychiatric ward for acute emotional problems served at least twenty-four children with temporary but intensive treatment. A family living seminar offering on-going preventive education for parents who want to better understand their role in promoting family mental health is conducted regularly. A birth-defects clinic, a physical therapy department, a speech and hearing clinic, a pediatric respiratory care center, a brace department, and a dental clinic were all part of the center. School has always been held for long-term patients. Pre-admittance "lemonade parties" are held to acquaint soon-to-be patients with hospital procedures. "Teen-Happenings," a similar program for older children, is held weekly. Over one hundred volunteer "pink ladies" and one hundred "candy stripers" (sixteen-year-old girls) give hours of service each week.

For sixty-one years the Primary Association and the Children's Hospital were almost synonymous. One could not be thought of without the other. Having given up one favorite child, the *Children's Friend,* to which it had given birth and nurturance for sixty-nine years, the Primary had to relinquish another. It was a necessary but traumatic separation. No one felt its loss more personally than Sister Parmley, who had worked so closely with it for over twenty years. "I was there when they built this whole big new hospital, raised the money, and helped to work all the plans, and moved the children from the old hospital to the new hospital," she recalled. "It was just part of my life and I knew all those children and I've seen many of them out in the countries when I've visited and they were well and happy."[19] The hospital had been a unifying cause not only within the Church, but also without, bringing together otherwise disparate groups and individuals in a common humanitarian concern. In Salt Lake City, perhaps more than anywhere else, it touched the wellspring of the best in human nature at least once a year during the annual Primary Penny Parade.

In 1948, just six months before conditions made it possible for him to signal the beginning of construction of the new hospital, President George Albert Smith made the new hospital the subject of his Primary Conference address. He urged all who listened and Church members everywhere to make an investment in the new edifice. Then, recounting the history of the old convalescent home and the tremendous service it had performed in behalf of 5,907 children, he expressed his deepest hopes for the new structure, which he would not live to see completed. "When *He* looks down," he told the audience, "I hope that He will be able to say that the Primary Association of The Church of Jesus Christ of Latter-day Saints has built one of the finest of all the buildings to be found in the valley and one of those most precious to Him in all the world."

Thousands of grown-up Primary children remember marching to the tune of the Primary Penny Song and singing every word as they proudly dropped their coins into a small replica of the Children's Hospital:

> Five pennies make a nickel;
> Two nickels make a dime;
> Ten dimes will make a dollar,
> How we'll make it shine.
>
> It's for the crippled children
> Who cannot walk or run;
> Who have to lie in bed all day
> And cannot join our fun.
>
> So let us be unselfish
> And bring our pennies here
> To help the crippled children
> Become stronger year by year.
>
> Let's march along and sing our song,
> And pray that they may be
> A little better every day
> Because of you and me.[20]

It was never easy to carry the load of a project like a children's hospital. Sister Parmley often remarked that when she met Sister Felt and Sister Anderson someday she would tell them, "It was easier to have the dream than it was to run the hospital."[21] Nevertheless, when she learned that the Primary would no longer have responsibility for it, she said, "I don't think anything will ever be as tremendous as the Primary Children's Hospital when I

177

see what it has done for children all over the world....It was just the pinnacle of love."[22] Many could share Sister Parmley's feelings when she was told about the divestment of the hospital: "It has taken a great part of my life and now I have the feeling that I have lost something very, very precious to me."[23]

The Primary Children's Medical Center continues the superior medical treatment it has always provided, and will continue to depend upon the generous impulses of the community at large. But the special significance of children giving to other children "who cannot walk or run" came from the deep sense of identity that one child had with another, instilled in them through this program of the Primary. The Primary Children's Hospital must stand as one of the proud achievements in the history of this organization.

Primary Children's Hospital, Salt Lake City, Utah

Primary children's parade, centennial celebration,
Church Office Building, August 11, 1978

Chapter Ten

"I Love Primary"

As Primary moved into its second century in August 1978, it could look back to a grand conclusion of its first. The one-hundredth-year celebration was a twelve-month affair. Unlike the fiftieth anniversary, where the major celebration was held in Salt Lake City involving 12,000 children, the hundredth anniversary was celebrated in wards and stakes, branches and districts all over the world, by half a million children. Special sacrament meetings and stake conference sessions made note of the anniversary, and Primary classes adapted their parties and activities to fit the great occasion. Pageants, skits, and programs in many languages told the story of the first Primary. But the big event in many of the Primaries was the old-fashioned fair, patterned after the fairs Sister Rogers and the early Primaries held to display and sell children's handiwork. During the summer Primaries throughout the Church held their own fairs with games, refreshments, and exhibits. Banners of red, yellow, and blue, the Primary colors, floating atop the booths or pinned to the walls, announced the celebration, and replicas of the little rock church in Farmington appeared in crayon, poster paint, watercolor, clay, and cardboard and even in delightfully decorated cakes. Primary children in Mexico, Germany, and Korea, no less than those in the American West, learned well the beginning of their association.

The Primary had indeed come far since its first meeting in Farmington in 1878. Originally organized to turn unruly boys into little gentlemen, it entered its second century reinforced by a strong network of correlated Church programs translated into seventeen languages, all directed toward the spiritual development of every LDS child. The programs of the Primary and the Sunday School have been coordinated to ensure that they reinforce rather than duplicate each other. Primaries for the handicapped are now part of a larger Church program developed to assist all members with special needs. A special committee produces basic lessons for developing areas, which are often newly formed branches and sometimes family or small area groups. These lessons are designed for children from six to twelve, for teachers who have never taught before, and for places where no Church facilities or teaching aids are available. Other Church programs whose concern is children also support the Primary and Sunday School, whose specific charge is to teach the gospel to the estimated 700,000 Latter-day Saint children under the age of twelve. The family home evening program provides opportunities for children to learn in a family setting the same concepts, in different versions, that they are taught in Sunday School and Primary. Mother education lessons in Relief Society, instruction for fathers in priesthood lessons, and special adult Sunday School lessons assist parents in teaching their children. The *Friend* continues to augment gospel teachings for children through stories, poems, and activities that reflect the realities of life. In addition, the Child Correlation Review Committee has been organized to review all material produced for children in the Church.

With the broad range of help that can come from a Church-backed rather than an auxiliary-supported program, the Primary has been able to expand its influence into the lives of every teachable child. "The spirit of correlation," Elder Boyd K. Packer told Primary workers in conference in 1970, "is the spirit of unity."[1] When Aurelia Rogers assembled the children of Farmington one hundred years ago, she knew what her purpose was, but she was almost alone in determining how to meet the needs of those children sitting before her. There is not a single Primary worker in the Church today, however, on any level or in any situation who cannot obtain some measure of help in meeting the purposes of her calling.

President Parmley oversaw the changes that occurred in rapid succession during her last years as president. As it relinquished responsibility for the Primary Children's Hospital and the *Children's Friend* and sole responsibility for planning and writing lesson manuals, the Primary took its place beside the other auxiliaries in a priesthood-directed and correlated program. The transfer of the hospital and the magazine to other agencies released time and effort to be directed wholly to the implementation of the spiritual educational program of the Primary on an expanding worldwide basis. From a high of seventy board members, the Primary presently functions with thirty.

Naomi M. Shumway, like her predecessor, brings many years of experience to her call as the sixth general president of the Primary. She served as both ward and stake Primary president before her assignment to the general board in 1963, and served eleven years on the board before she was appointed general president in 1974. She was born in Provo, Utah, on October 3, 1922, a daughter of Albert E. and Orilla May Brown Maxfield. Before marrying Roden G. Shumway in 1945, she attended business college. Continuing a precedent set by Sister Parmley, she has been active in Scouting, serving as a member of the National Cub Scout Committee and a member of the executive board of the Great Salt Lake Council of the Boy Scouts of America. She also received the Silver Fawn award from the Boy Scouts.

As a member of the Primary general board, Sister Shumway saw the broad changes of responsibility that occurred in the early 1970s and was prepared to lead the Primary in meeting the challenges that the worldwide program presented. Sometimes called "a gentle giant" by her board members because of the effective combination of her gentle manner and giant capacity and dedication, Sister Shumway has brought her own style of leadership to the Primary.

When called to preside over this far-reaching children's organization, Sister Shumway was told by President Kimball that she now had responsibility for every Primary child. That awesome charge infused this gentle, refined lady with an intensity and determination to meet and even exceed every expectation of her calling. Well-organized, diligent, and completely committed to the Primary program, she understands the breadth of her stewardship and sets a clear direction for her co-workers to follow. Often reminding her board members that Primary is designed "to train, not entertain" children, she challenges them to justify their suggestions and program ideas against the standard of spiritually strengthening every child. Her message to Primary workers has always been to "catch the vision of Primary," a vision that her dedication demonstrates was long ago incised in her own mind and heart. A critical illness of her only son many years ago is likely the source of the particular love and tenderness she feels toward the young Primary boys; and like her predecessor, who grew up with eight brothers, she has made the boys' program her specialty. The boys' program is her assigned responsibility as president, but her knowledge of and concern for the whole program motivates her meticulous supervision of all that is part of Primary. Sister Shumway is supported by two able counselors, Colleen B. Lemmon and Dorthea C. Murdock (who replaced Sara B. Paulsen in 1977).

Behind the inspired and devoted women who have served the little Saints as general Primary presidents have been the priesthood leaders who have served as their advisers for most of the first hundred years. In the beginning Eliza R. Snow, as general Relief Society president, acted as liaison between the brethren and the women's auxiliaries, but Louie B. Felt and May Anderson had only an informal association with some of the General Authorities. The appointment of advisers in 1909 made the channel of communication with priesthood leaders thus more directly accessible to auxiliary heads. Of the many brethren who served in this capacity, none served longer with the Primary than Elder Harold B. Lee and Elder Marion G. Romney, appointed by President Grant in 1943 because, as he told Brother Romney rather good-humoredly, he "wanted men a little nearer the children's age than the previous advisers."[2] These two men served twenty years as Primary advisers, personally setting apart new board members, attending hospital board meetings and general board meetings, and speaking regularly at Primary conferences. Serving at a time when the Church was still largely Utah-centered, they were able to counsel often with the two presidents who served with them, Sister Howells and Sister Parmley, and to develop lasting friendships with board members.

Until recent times, when the growth of the Church no longer permits either the time or the proximity, Primary presidents, like other auxiliary leaders, were able to develop personal friendships along with official relationships with their presiding brethren, and much of the work of the Primary was decided in informal settings. Both Sister Hinckley and Sister Howells were close friends of President Grant before their appointment to the Primary, and his personal as well as official support was greatly beneficial. Currently, priesthood advisers serve for shorter periods and with less direct personal involvement, inasmuch as correlation and reorganization programs assume much of the responsibility once held solely by the advisers. At the time of the 1978 Primary centennial, all of the youth programs came under the priesthood supervision of an executive director, with a specific managing director, Elder Robert L. Backman, serving with the Primary.

In a message to Primary workers at their annual conference in April 1948, Elder Romney described the relationship of advisers and other leaders with those whom they serve:

> I want to say at the outset that I am very grateful for the fact that Brother Lee and Brother Moyle [members of the Council of Twelve] have come over to this session and will listen to what I have to say. One of the sweetest things in my experience is the loyalty and the support that these two men give to me. They are my file leaders, not only in Primary but also in my welfare work where I am assigned to labor a good part of the time. We do a lot of praying in the Church for the leaders. We who are in the under positions pray that the Lord will sustain the leaders, and we sustain them with our work. But the leaders also sustain those whom they lead. I wish you could have, in every stake and in every organization

of the Primary work, the kind of loyalty and support from the leader to the person whom he or she leads that I have from my file leaders.

As Primary attempts to touch the lives of every Latter-day Saint child throughout the world, as well as many who are not members, its programs are translated and adapted to suit a variety of circumstances, for all of the lessons and activities are carefully planned with one goal: to teach children the gospel. Women dedicated to that obligation, with supportive priesthood leaders, have made the program work and bear fruit under incredibly difficult situations. One such worker in Liege, Belgium, Sister Jeanine W. Marichal, grew in understanding, ability, and confidence along with the Primary program she nurtured in a country far from the center of the Church. Expressing thanks for some encouraging letters from a general board member who visited her area in 1972, she found the letters "comforting to us who are still pioneers in Europe. We must sow a lot to harvest a little. Our home Primaries and our young investigators are the proof thereof."[3] Later she expressed a feeling shared by many Primary workers: "I like my Primaries. I feel like I have adopted all these little children and like I am the older sister of all my Primary officers.... What a big FAMILY!"[4] Her feelings reflect those of a much earlier pioneer Primary worker, Eliza R. Snow, who called the children of Cache Valley, where she was visiting, "all hers" and told them "she loved them all."[5] To another group she said, "Now my darling children, I call you mine because I love you so much. You won't object to my calling you my children, will you?"[6] For the many childless women who have worked in Primary, like Eliza R. Snow, Louie B. Felt, May Anderson, and May Green Hinckley, the children have indeed become their special care and the program has benefited from their service to it.

Primary in Belgium, as in any pioneering area, met difficulties. Transportation and places to meet posed the largest problems, and inexperienced Primary workers were not always able to implement the program easily. Yet shortly before the district became a stake,

Sister Marichal was able to report that "the work is advancing and the programs are in full swing."[7] Her commitment to the program was evident in a letter she wrote to her friend on the Primary general board: "We are all aware of the value of a child in the eyes of our Heavenly Father, and we know that we must not stop as long as there are children who thirst and hunger for the Gospel and the love of Christ; we find it often in our little investigators at Primary who are still living in darkness while it is noon, and this is our greatest desire: 'That they might know thee the only true God.'"[8]

Across the world in Japan the modern-day pioneering continues. When transportation became an almost insurmountable problem in one Japanese branch, the Primary officers visited the parents and found several mothers who had access to automobiles but did not know how to drive. With the help of the home teachers, the Primary officers taught the mothers to drive and then requested their husbands to take the bus to work on Saturdays so that the mothers could bring their children to Primary. Not only did the children now have a way to get to Primary, but their mothers became teachers as well![9]

In another Japanese branch, a fifteen-year-old girl was chosen to be Primary president. She had no supplies and little help to begin with except that of the missionaries who told her of their Primary experiences. So she made a slide picture show from Bible stories for lessons and taught Japanese dances for activity, carrying on the Primary herself until she obtained the interest and help of parents. Later, when she was appointed stake Primary president, some questioned the suitability of a single woman without children taking the responsibility of the Primary. When the stake president asked, "Kyoko, you love children, don't you?" she quickly answered, "Of course, I love every child. My love is second to none." Knowing that love of children is not restricted to mothers, as many Primary workers have well proved, the astute stake president assured Kyoko that she was "well worth the work of Primary." Like her Belgian counterpart, this young Japanese woman felt the bonds of sisterhood among the women who worked in Primary. She looked to the general Primary president (who was then Sister Parmley) as a "beloved mother," and the general board members from Salt Lake City who visited her while she served as "special big sisters."[10]

When Aurelia Rogers requested an organization to help train little boys to become better men, she was issuing a cry for help. Responding as a mother to the challenges of rearing children to become responsible adults, she was searching for sources of help in that awesome responsibility. Her plea reverberated throughout the territory, and women responded to what was more than just one woman's concern. In a union of purpose they brought their individual parenting skills to a new collective venture, and together they prayerfully interpreted the needs of children and how best to meet them. Years later, in 1947, President David O. McKay told a group of Primary workers, "The parent gives the child an opportunity to live," and "the teacher enables the child to live well." But, he continued, "the parent who gives life and teaches his child to live abundantly is a true parent-teacher."[11] As teachers in the Primary from its beginning, mother have been able to augment their parental teaching responsibilities in the home with well-planned programs in the Primary. Moreover, their children have been the beneficiaries of the teaching of concerned women other than their own mothers.

A hundred years after Aurelia Rogers first expressed her desire for an organization to help parents train their children, general Primary president Naomi Shumway enunciated the Primary's need for parents to help the Primary: "We need you to work with us in teaching your children the gospel.... Our greatest concern is your child's spiritual growth, and we need you.... We love your children. Please keep sending them to us."[12] In very deed the Primary is serving the function it has always earmarked for itself—partnership with parents.

Over the years children have found their own ways to express their love for Primary. In 1889 the Primary children of the Logan

Sixth Ward gave their president a surprise party on her birthday with a picnic lunch, a birthday cake, and a special gift of a pair of window curtains.[13] The children of the Kaysville (Utah) Primary also showed appreciation for their Primary president, Jane Blood, by celebrating her birthday with a surprise party introduced by the entire group of two hundred children singing Primary songs in her front yard. After refreshments, which had been prepared by the children, were served, the organ was moved from Sister Blood's parlor to her porch, and the children, the neighbors, and Sister Blood and her family all sang Primary songs and hymns. The party concluded with a poem dedicated to Sister Blood:

> Dear Sister Blood, you're happier I know
> Than a queen on her throne could be.
> You're surrounded with gems more precious than gold,
> A sight most delightful to see.
>
> Two hundred children have met here today,
> To sing you sweet songs of love,
> To cheer you and bless you and make your heart glad,
> As you journey to mansions above.
>
> Two hundred hearts beating joyfully here,
> Bound by love's sweet cords that are strong.
> They ne'er will be broken while time shall endure,
> Then they'll meet you in Heaven's bright throng.[14]

Another Primary president was honored in a different way. When the bishop of the Logan (Utah) Second Ward decided to release Ruth Hatch Hale, the Primary president, for another ward assignment and put the proposal before the ward congregation for a sustaining vote, not a hand was raised in approval. Sister Hale was so well loved by the children and their parents that they were not willing to give her up to another organization.[15]

Perhaps one of the most elaborate displays of the children's affection and reverence for the Church and especially for Church leaders in early days was given to President Lorenzo Snow. The Primary children of the entire Salt Lake Valley were invited to attend general conference and meet President Snow. In honor of this memorable occasion, all of the little Primary girls dressed in white dresses with colored sashes and with matching ribbons in their hair. At the appropriate time the multitude of white-clad little girls, interspersed with cleanly scrubbed little boys in their Sunday suits, walked up the north aisle of the Salt Lake Tabernacle, across the stand where the brethren were seated, and down the south aisle to the back of the building. Each child carried a rose. As the children passed President Snow, each one laid a rose on his lap and shook his hand. One little girl remembered that "when my turn came to greet him I could hardly see him for the roses."[16]

In the Primary's centennial year, following the April 1978 conference, a similar moving tribute was paid to President Spencer W. Kimball during a special program in the twenty-sixth floor auditorium of the Church Office Building in Salt Lake City. President Kimball recalled for the children, the Primary general presidency, and the General Authorities and their wives his own memories of Primary and its tremendous opportunities for the future. Afterward everyone joined in singing "I Am a Child of God" to conclude a special program in honor of the Primary's centennial year.

During the centennial celebration of the Primary, Sister Shumway was asked if she felt there had been great changes in the Primary during its first hundred years. Her answer was significant: "The program today is essentially the same as always. The needs of children are still the same as they were a hundred years ago, even though they might be met in different ways. Primary is just in more places with more children."

Two letters from two young Primary boys support Sister Shumway's assessment. The first is from Thomas Pike of Logan, written in 1881:

I belong to the 5th Ward Primary Association of Logan and I love to go for we have such good meetings, and we have our President Priscilla Jacobs and her Counselors Mary Kent and Mary Adams, they are so good and kind to us, they come every Saturday and some of our fathers and mothers. They give us many good instructions and sing us good songs, we learn many good things. I am only a little boy 8 years and 2 months old today but I am a Mormon boy and never drink tea nor coffee....[17]

The second is from a young Primary boy in Japan, written in 1978:

I love Primary. In Primary we study the gospel and learn the things that are good for us and also the activity time. We also can prepare to receive the priesthood and honor it. In Primary we find friends. We learn the Articles of Faith and scriptures and learn to apply them so that we can receive the great blessings of the priesthood. I think the things we learn in Primary will be a great help when I will go on a mission. I would like to be a good missionary and want to tell many people about Heavenly Father's gospel.[18]

Though many years apart in time and many miles apart in distance, the two letters indicate that Primary has indeed touched its young charges with a love of their organization and an understanding and appreciation of the gospel. Primary children have responded to the love and efforts of thousands of women who have taken seriously the injunction to teach the gospel to the little Saints. The trust given to these devoted women by President John Taylor a century ago was reiterated by President Spencer W. Kimball when he was an apostle in 1949. To the Primary leaders assembled in conference of that year he said: "I almost envy the sisters who have the privilege of working with the children, these little folks who are still moldable clay in your hands, children whose minds are unfettered by the sophistries of the world, children who have not had their faith spoiled, children who can still believe and have an unadulterated faith. You have a great privilege to work with these people."[19]

Whatever the second century holds for the Primary, its first stands as a monument to a host of dedicated sisters who understood the worth of the little Saints put in their charge and did their best to "polish...refine...and prepare [them] to stand in the diadem of their Father's crown."[20]

Top left: Primary general board officers, circa 1900. Seated: Louie B. Felt; standing: Aurelia Spencer Rogers, May Anderson. Top right: May Green Hinckley. Bottom left to right: Adele Cannon Howells, LaVern Watts Parmley, Naomi M. Shumway.

Appendix 1

General Presidents and Counselors

President Louie B. Felt
(June 19, 1880-October 6, 1925)
First Counselor:

Matilda M. Barratt (June 19, 1880-October 1888)

Lillie T. Freeze (October 1888-December 8, 1905)

May Anderson (December 29, 1905-October 6, 1925)

Second Counselor:

Clara C. M. Cannon (June 19, 1880-October 4, 1895)

Josephine R. West (December 15, 1896-November 24, 1905)

Clara W. Beebe (December 29, 1905-October 6, 1925)

President May Anderson
(October 6, 1925-September 11, 1939)
First Counselor:

Sadie Grant Pack (October 6, 1925-September 11, 1929)

Isabelle Salmon Ross (September 11, 1929-December 31, 1939)

Second Counselor:

Isabelle Salmon Ross (October 6, 1925-September 11, 1929)

Edna Harker Thomas (September 11, 1929-December 1, 1933)

Edith Hunter Lambert (December 1, 1933-December 31, 1939)

President May Green Hinckley
(January 1, 1940-May 2, 1943)
First Counselor:

Adele Cannon Howells (January 1, 1940-May 2, 1943)

Second Counselor:

Janet Murdock Thompson (January 1, 1940-March 1942)

LaVern Watts Parmley (March 1942-May 2, 1943)

President Adele Cannon Howells
(July 20, 1943-April 14, 1951)

First Counselor:

LaVern Watts Parmley (July 20, 1943-April 14, 1951)

Second Counselor:

Dessie Grant Boyle (July 20, 1943-April 14, 1951)

President LaVern Watts Parmley
(May 16, 1951-October 5, 1974)

First Counselor:

Arta M. Hale (May 16, 1951-April 6, 1962)

Leone W. Doxey (April 6, 1962-October 23, 1969)

Lucile C. Reading (January 8, 1970-August 6, 1970)

Naomi W. Randall (October 4, 1970-October 5, 1974)

Second Counselor:

Florence H. Richards (May 16, 1951-June 11, 1953)

Leone W. Doxey (September 10, 1953-April 6, 1962)

Eileen R. Dunyon (April 6, 1962-June 3, 1963)

Lucile C. Reading (July 23, 1963-January 8, 1970)

Florence R. Lane (January 8, 1970-October 5, 1974)

President Naomi M. Shumway
(October 5, 1974-   )

First Counselor:

Sara B. Paulsen (October 5, 1974-April 2, 1977)

Colleen B. Lemmon (April 2, 1977-   )

Second Counselor:

Colleen B. Lemmon (October 5, 1974-April 2, 1977)

Dorthea C. Murdock (April 2, 1977-   )

Appendix 2

Members of the Primary
General Board, 1880-1978

Louie B. Felt
1880-1925

Ivy Allen (1911-1917)
May Anderson (1890-1939; 1905-1926,
  counselor; 1925-1939, president)
Matilda M. Barratt (1880-1888,
  counselor)
Clara W. Beebe (1904-1927; 1905-1925,
  counselor)
Eliza S. Bennion (1901-1934)
Stella P. Bradford (1913-never able to
  serve)
Euphemia I. Burnham (1896-1906)
Matilda W. Cahoon (1913-1939)
Rose Canfield (1892-1895)
Clara M. Cannon (1880-1896; 1880-
  1895, counselor)
Ella S. Capener (1913-1923)
Zina Y. Card (1906-1911; 1918-1921)
Jennie Careless (1904-date indefinite)
Olive Derbridge Christensen (1897-
  1901)
Cornelia H. Clayton (1895-1901)
Camilla S. Cobb (1898-1917)
Jane R. Crawford (1919-1938)
Florence Critchlow (1906-1907)
Minnie Felt Cutler (1880-1890)
Helen Davis (1913-1939)
Genet Bingham Dee (1916-1939)
Margaret Hull Eastmond (1904-1917)
Edna C. Ericksen (1920-1939)

Beatrice Cannon Evans (1913-date
  indefinite)
Irma Bitner Evans (1911-date indefinite)
Vera I. Felt (1904-date indefinite)
Norma Fenton (1904-1909)
Grace Folland (1904-1907)
Lillie T. Freeze (1888-1905, counselor)
Marjorie Gowans (1924-1926)
Adelaide U. E. Hardy (1913-1917; 1928-
  1938)
Annie K. Hardy (1896-1899)
Alice Howarth (1906-1917)
Sarah E. Hyde (1892-1901)
Mary R. Jack (1920-1939)
Edna Evans Johnson (1917-1917)
Marion Belnap Kerr (1914-1939)
Edith Hunter Lambert (1910-1939;
  1934-1939, counselor)
Lillian L. Maeser (1904-1906)
Effie Howe Mellor (1910-1910)
Amy Lyman Merrill (1910-1913)
Zaidie Walker Miles (1895-1900)
Annie S. Milne (1913-1917)
Emma Ramsey Morris (1910-date
  indefinite)
Ann Nebeker (1910-1939)
Julie Ivins Pace (date indefinite-death,
  1900)
Sadie Grant Pack (1918-1929; 1925-
  1929, counselor)
Vilate Peart (1906-death, 1909)
Laura L. Foster Phelps (1910-1919)

195

Vilate S. Chambers Raile (1913-1931)

Eleanor R. Jeremy Richards (1913-1919)

Georgina F. Richards (1913-1927)

Lula L. Greene Richards (before 1892-1917)

Aurelia S. Rogers (1893-death, 1922)

Emma P. Romney (1906-1917)

Isabelle S. Ross (1892-1939; 1925-1939, counselor)

Myrtle B. Shurtliff (1912-1913)

Cordia H. Smith (1917-1939)

Edna L. Smith (1901-1911)

Ida B. Smith (1902-death, 1918)

Josephine G. Smith (1903-1905)

Alice T. Sheets Smoot (1920-1930)

Minnie Loveland Snow (1904-1906)

Ella Nebeker Stewart (1892-1899)

Emily S. Stewart (1920-1931)

Lucy Stringham (1906-1907)

Florence Summerhays (1913-1917)

Nelle A. Talmage (1916-1927)

Edna H. Thomas (1904-1934; 1929-1934, counselor)

Eleanor B. Thomas (1922-1935)

Francis K. Thomassen (1910-1918)

Anne Wallace (1904-1907)

Josephine R. West (1893-1905; 1896-1905, counselor)

Rebecca Nibley Whitney (1906-1912)

Maria B. Winder (1906-1911)

Fanny Woolley (1903-date indefinite)

Afton Young (1920-1939)

Emmeline McMaster Young (1906-date indefinite)

Mary I. Young (1913-1917)

May Anderson
1925-1939

Vesta E. Anderson (1936-1956)

Clara W. Beebe (1904-1927)

Glenn J. Beeley (1926-1929)

Frances G. Bennett (1936-1942; 1945-1952)

Eliza S. Bennion (1901-1934)

Katherine S. Bennion (1936-1942)

Maurine Bennion (1926-1928)

Jennie Campbell (1937-1951)

Lenore Cornwall (1932-1937)

Jane R. Crawford (-1939)

Matilda W. Cahoon (1913-1939)

Helen Davis (1913-1939)

Ina Harris Day (1937-1939)

Genet Bingham Dee (1916-1939)

Edna C. Ericksen (1920-1939)

Marjorie Gowans (1924-1926)

Adelaide U. E. Hardy (1928-)

Ruth W. Higginbotham (1939-1942)

Berniece A. Ivory (1932-1943)

Mary R. Jack (1920-1939)

Wilma Jeppson (1936-1939)

Marion Belnap Kerr (1914-1939)

Edith Hunter Lambert (1910-1939; 1933-1939, counselor)

Ebba P. Larson (1932-1943)

Phyllis L. Leishman (1932-1943)

Leah A. Lloyd (1936-1956)

Ann Nebeker (1910-1939)

Sadie Grant Pack (1918-1929)

Mildred T. Pettit (1932-1936)

Georgina F. Richards (1913-1927)

Isabella S. Ross (1892-1939; 1929-1939, counselor)

Bessie Jones Schettler (1929-1943)

Jessie Schofield (1938-1944)

Cordia H. Smith (1917-1939)

Gertrude P. Smith (1929-1939)

Ruth P. Smith (1929-1947)

Alice T. Sheets Smith (1920-1930)

Emily S. Stewart (1920-1931)

Margaret H. Stromness (1938-1956)

Nelle A. Talmage (1916-1927)

Edna H. Thomas (1904-1933; 1929-1933, counselor)

Eleanor B. Thomas (1922-1935)

Grace D. Wahlquist (1938-1944)

Vera P. Wahlquist (1929-1943)

Josephine R. West (1893-1905)

LaDell Lowry Woolley (1935-1942)

Afton Young (1920-1939)

May Green Hinckley
1940-1943

Vesta E. Anderson (1936-1956)
Frances G. Bennett (1936-1942;
  1945-1952)
Katherine S. Bennion (1936-1942)
Dessie G. Boyle (1942-1956; 1943-
  1951, counselor)
Zina C. Brockbank (1942-1964)
Olga C. Brown (1940-1964)
Jennie Campbell (1937-1951)
Ruth B. Coon (1940-1945)
Fern C. Eyring (1940-1946)
Nina Halliday (1941-1954)
Ruth W. Higginbotham (1939-1942)
Adele Cannon Howells (1940-1951;
  1940-1943, counselor; 1943-1951,
  president)
Berniece A. Ivory (1932-1943)
Ebba P. Larson (1932-1943)
Phyllis L. Leishman (1932-1943)
Leah A. Lloyd (1936-1956)
Alta Miller (1942-1974)
LaVern Watts Parmley (1941-1974;
  1942-1951, counselor; 1951-1974,
  president)
Beth Paxman (1940-1940)
Bertha S. Reeder (1941-1943)
Bessie Jones Schettler (1929-1943,
  secretary)
Jessie Schofield (1938-1944)
Ruth P. Smith (1929-1947)
Margaret H. Stromness (1938-1956)
Janet Murdock Thompson (1940-
  1942, counselor)
Grace D. Wahlquist (1938-1944)
Vera P. Wahlquist (1929-1943)
Beatrice Winsor (1942-1952)
Villetta C. Wood (1942-1956)
LaDell L. Woolley (1935-1942)

Adele Cannon Howells
1943-1951

Vesta E. Anderson (1936-1956)

Frances G. Bennett (1936-1942; 1945-
  1952)
Zina C. Brockbank (1942-1964)
Olga C. Brown (1940-1964)
Dessie Grant Boyle (1942-1956;
  1943-1951, counselor)
Wilma B. Bunker (1947-1948;
  1959-1966)
Jennie Campbell (1937-1951)
Don Etta June Carlisle (1950-1970)
Ruth Chadwick (1944-1954)
Ruth B. Coon (1940-1945)
Leone P. Cowley (1944-1951)
Fern Dansie (1945-1946)
Bernice A. Einzinger (1951-1970)
Fern C. Eyring (1940-1946)
Edna M. Faux (1947-1972)
Mary B. Firmage (1946-1953)
Arta M. Hale (1945-1962; 1951-1962,
  counselor)
Nina Halliday (1941-1954)
Elaine P. Handley (1946-1947)
Sybil W. Hansen (1951-1967)
Thelma J. Harrison (1945-1950; 1963-
  1974)
Lillian Jensen (1943-1944)
Norma F. Knight (1949-1961)
Velma H. Lindsay (1947-1953)
Dixie P. Lloyd (1944-1950)
Leah A. Lloyd (1936-1956)
Ardella R. Lowry (1945-1961)
Hermana F. Lyon (1944-1962)
LaVern Watts Parmley (1942-1974;
  1942-1951, counselor; 1951-1974,
  president)
Mary P. Parrish (1944-1964)
Edith S. Patrick (1944-1964)
Tessie G. Post (1947-1960)
Naomi W. Randall (1947-1974)
Angie V. Rawlins (1942-1949)
Catharine A. Rich (1951-1971)
Florence H. Richards (1946-1953;
  1951-1953, counselor)
Jessie Schofield (1938-1951)
Phyllis H. Shorten (1949-1964)

197

Ruth P. Smith (1941-1947)
Delsa P. Stevens (1947-1961)
Margaret H. Stromness (1938-1956)
Grace D. Wahlquist (1938-1944)
Fern F. Whipple (1947-1964)
Beatrice S. Winsor (1942-1952)
Villetta C. Wood (1942-1956)

LaVern Watts Parmley
1951-1974

Faye S. Aagaard (1965-1970)
Helen H. Alldredge (1961-1970)
Marie R. Anderson (1969-1969)
Regena J. Anderson (1952-1956)
Vesta E. Anderson (1936-1956)
Virginia W. Anderson (1966-1974)
Marion E. Astin (1959-1974)
Anna F. Bailey (1970-1975)
Reta D. Baldwin (1969-   )
Mary S. Bankhead (1970-1974)
Frances G. Bennett (1936-1942; 1945-1952)
Beatrice R. Berg (1970-1974)
Drucilla S. Bott (1965-1968)
Orpha S. Boyden (1952-1963)
Dessie Grant Boyle (1942-1956; 1943-1951, counselor)
Lorna S. Broadbent (1956-1960)
Mary Lou Broadbent (1965-1970)
Zina C. Brockbank (1942-1964)
Olga C. Brown (1940-1964)
Virginia C. Bryner (1967-1973)
Wilma B. Bunker (1947-1948; 1959-1966)
Beulah D. Burgoyne (1971-   )
Minnie P. Burton (1961-1966)
LauRene T. Buswell (1965-1974)
Jennie Campbell (1937-1951)
Marjorie S. Cannon (1962-1972)
Virginia B. Cannon (1967-   )
Don Etta June Carlisle (1950-1970)
Amy M. Casto (1956-1970)
Ruth Chadwick (1944-1954)
Susan R. Christensen (1971-1974)
Lucy L. Clark (1970-1974)

Edna B. Clawson (1962-1966)
Catherine M. Clement (1965-1966)
Ruth C. Clinger (1963-1970)
Leone P. Cowley (1944-1951)
Ruth Jane Dall (1967-1974)
Beth S. Davey (1956-1970)
Thelma B. deJong (1953-1967)
Gladys H. Densley (1967-1970)
Carmen M. Dibble (1970-1975)
Fulvia Dixon (1970-   )
Lucille A. Douglas (1952-1957)
Leone W. Doxey (1953-1966, counselor)
Mary C. Dunn (1963-1974)
Eileen R. Dunyon (1956-1967; 1962-1963, counselor)
Catherine E. Edwards (1961-1962)
Bernice A. Einzinger (1951-1970)
Claudia Jean F. Eliason (1972-   )
Amy L. Engar (1965-1974)
LaNore D. Espenshied (1970-   )
Helen B. Evans (1951-1968)
Emma J. Farnsworth (1967-1974)
Edna M. Faux (1947-1972)
Thelma W. Fetzer (1963-   )
Mary B. Firmage (1946-1953)
Camille de St. Jeor Gambles (1973-   )
Erma Y. Gardiner (1959-1962)
Ruth M. Gardner (1971-   )
Kathlyn F. Garff (1962-1970)
Kathryn S. Gilbert (1953-1963)
Marie M. Glade (1966-1974)
Adena Nell S. Gourley (1961-1970)
Ruby O. Haight (1967-1971)
Arta M. Hale (1945-1962; 1951-1962, counselor)
Lucile F. Hales (1965-1965)
Nina Halliday (1941-1954)
Myrl W. Hamilton (1956-1974)
Sybil W. Hansen (1951-1967)
Thelma J. Harrison (1945-1950; 1963-1974)
Helen Beth Henrichsen (1953-1965)
Annie O. Hiller (1960-1965)
Jeanne M. Hughes (1965-1974)
Maurine M. Hughes (1967-1974)

Ramona M. Jacob (1966-1974)
Agnes S. Jacobs (1965-1974)
Vauna S. Jacobsen (1953-1970)
Carolyn Jensen (1958-1958)
Mary Jane E. Johnson (1967-   )
Sarah L. Johnson (1956-1967)
Mercedes R. Iverson Kiepe (1971-1974)
Marjorie C. Kjar (1970-1975)
Norma F. Knight (1949-1961)
Erma A. Kunzler (1969-1974)
Florence R. Lane (1967-1974; 1970-
    1974, counselor)
Jeanne J. Larson (1973-   )
Lou S. Groesbeck Law (1954-1974)
Freda Joan J. Lee (1963-1974)
Colleen B. Lemmon (1971-1974;
    1974-   , counselor)
Trilba J. Lindsay (1963-   )
Velma H. Lindsay (1947-1953)
Leah A. Lloyd (1936-1956)
Ardella R. Lowry (1945-1961)
Ruth H. Lundgren (1970-   )
Hermana F. Lyon (1944-1962)
Patricia C. Maughan (1969-   )
Ada B. Maxfield (1953-1970)
Mildred C. McKay (1944-1956)
Clara W. McMaster (1956-1970)
Phyllis B. McMullin (1973-   )
Blanche B. Miles (1966-   )
Alta Miller (1942-1974)
Elva Killian Miller (1947-1956)
Claire T. Murdock (1952-1953)
Dorthea C. Murdock (1967-   ;
    1977-   , counselor)
Norma O. Nichols (1956-1970)
Mayre N. Nielsen (1959-1974)
Margaret P. Ottosen (1962-1974)
Judith W. Parker (1959-1974)
Darlene S. Parkinson (1958-1970)
Mary P. Parrish (1944-1964)
Edith S. Patrick (1944-1964)
Sara B. Paulsen (1970-1977; 1974-
    1977, counselor)
Alene R. Pettit (1965-1966)
Tessie G. Post (1947-1960)

Bertha B. Proctor (1956-1970)
Della D. Provost (1959-1962)
Naomi W. Randall (1947-1974)
Della Mae I. Rasmussen (1967-   )
Lucile C. Reading (1962-1970; 1963-
    1970, counselor)
Kathleen E. Reese (1972-1975)
Catharine A. Rich (1951-1971)
Edith Rich (1957-1970)
Florence H. Richards (1946-1953; 1951-
    1953, counselor)
Ruby O. Richards (1963-1966)
Patricia P. Romney (1962-1972)
Thelma J. Ryser (1954-1964)
Johanna V. Sharnborg (1954-1959)
Phyllis H. Shorten (1949-1964)
Carolyn B. Shumway (1969-death, 1972)
Naomi M. Shumway (1963-   ;
    1974-   , president)
Knell S. Skidmore (1962-1974)
Helene K. Smith (1966-1974)
Joe Ann Smith (1958-1965)
Mary Ellen S. Smith (1962-1970)
Norma B. Smith (1969-1974)
Olive L. Smith (1962-1966)
Barbara M. Smoot (1967-1974)
Katheryn J. Soelberg (1957-1964)
Minnie B. Sorensen (1953-1968)
Delsa P. Stevens (1947-1961)
Margaret H. Stromness (1938-1956)
Nedra H. Strong (1967-1970)
Blanche D. Sundberg (1954-1959)
Grace P. Swinyard (1963-1964)
Marilyn W. Taggart (1967-1974)
Dorothy B. Taylor (1972-   )
Lucelle R. Taylor (1956-1963)
Lucy C. D. Taylor (1956-1970)
Thelma B. Tovey (1961-1971)
Ada S. Van Dam (1956-1964)
Gwen S. Ward (1961-1970)
Donna S. Waters (1970-   )
Vanja Y. Watkins (1963-1970)
Fern F. Whipple (1947-1963)
Lurene G. Wilkinson (1962-1968)
Beatrice S. Winsor (1942-1952)

Yvonne W. Wiser (1952-1953)
Villetta C. Wood (1942-1956)
Dorothy N. Woodruff (1972-1974)
Helen G. Wright (1970-1974)
Marvel M. Young (1965-1966; 1968-
  1972)
Dwan J. Young (1970-   )

Naomi M. Shumway
1974-

Anna F. Bailey (1970-1975)
Delpha A. Baird (1977-   )
Reta D. Baldwin (1969-   )
Beulah D. Burgoyne (1971-   )
Virginia B. Cannon (1967-   )
Carmen M. Dibble (1970-1975)
Fulvia Dixon (1970-   )
Claudia Jean E. Eliason (1972-   )
LaNore D. Espenschied (1970-   )
Thelma W. Fetzer (1963-   )
Camille de St. Jeor Gambles (1973-   )
Ruth M. Gardner (1971-   )
Michaelene P. Grassli (1975-   )
Kathryn C. Harris (1977-   )
Marion S. Harrison (1973-   )

Mary Jane E. Johnson (1967-   )
Marjorie C. Kjar (1970-1975)
Jeanne J. Larson (1973-   )
Colleen B. Lemmon (1971-   ;
  1974-   , counselor)
Trilba J. Lindsay (1963-   )
Ruth H. Lundgren (1970-   )
Virginia M. Marsh (1977-   )
Patricia C. Maughan (1969-   )
Phyllis B. McMullin (1973-   )
Blanche B. Miles (1966-   )
Dorthea C. Murdock (1967-1977;
  1977-   , counselor)
Elaine T. Naylor (1975-   )
Sara B. Paulsen (1970-1977; 1974-1977,
  counselor)
Janice M. Piccolo (1978-   )
Della Mae I. Rasmussen (1967-   )
Kathleen E. Reese (1972-1975)
Myrl B. Silcox (1975-   )
Lois C. Sprunt (1975-   )
Dorothy B. Taylor (1972-   )
Donna S. Waters (1970-   )
Carolyn O. Welling (1975-   )
Dwan J. Young (1970-   )

Appendix 3

Priesthood Advisers

George F. Richards (1909-date indefinite)
Hyrum M. Smith (1909-1913)
Anthony W. Ivins (1913-1926)
David O. McKay (1918-1935)
Sylvester Q. Cannon (1926-1943)
Alonzo A. Hinckley (1935-1937)
Charles A. Callis (1937-1943)
Harold B. Lee (1943-1963)
Marion G. Romney (1943-1963)
Howard W. Hunter (1963-1970)
William J. Critchlow, Jr. (1963-1969)
Robert L. Simpson (1963-1972)
Gordon B. Hinckley (1970-1972)
Thomas S. Monson (1972-1976)
Boyd K. Packer (1972-1975)
Marvin J. Ashton (1972-1975)
Bruce R. McConkie (1974-1975)
Mark E. Petersen (1975-1976)
Marion D. Hanks, Managing Director of Youth (1976-1978)
Robert P. Backman, Managing Director of Youth (1978-   )

Years	Class Names and Ages	Emblems or Symbols
1878	All Primary children taught as one class. Earliest Primaries included ages 6 to 14, but Eliza R. Snow later set ages from 4 to 14.	
January 1902	First *Children's Friend* published lessons for three grades. (For several years prior to 1902, grading was tried in some local Primaries.)	
1908-1909	Announced Dec. 1908 that three grades would be expanded to five. Implemented in 1909. All classes consisted of both boys & girls. Grade 1: 4 and 5 years. Grade 2: 6 and 7 years. Grade 3: 8 and 9 years. Grade 4: 10 and 11 years. Grade 5: 12 and 13 years.	
1913	Scouting program adopted by Church. Boys 12 and 13 transferred to YMMIA with option of remaining in Primary if not interested.	
1915	Boys in Grade 5, ages 12 and 13, separated from girls. (The term "grade" for Primary classes was gradually replaced by "group.")	
1922	Seagull program for girls introduced 1922. In 1923 they were divided into 2 groups: Jr. Seagull Girls: 12 years. Sr. Seagull Girls: 13 years.	Seagull pin for Jr. girls. Seagull emblem on felt for Sr. girls.
1925-1926	Trail Builder program for boys 10 and 11 inaugurated.	Pine tree.
January 1926	Bluebird Group began for girls 10-11 years of age.	Enameled bluebird pin.

Class Names, Emblems, Colors, and Mottoes
By Anna Mae Robison, Library, Church Historical Department

Colors	Mottoes or Codes	
	"I am, I can, I ought, I will."	
Silver or white plus harmonizing color chosen by stake.	"Serve Gladly."	
Green and brown.	"I'll strive to do my best; To be loyal to my Heavenly Father, To honor my parents, To obey tribe rules, And to serve every day." (1925.)	
Blue and white.	"Happiness and Service." (1926.)	

Years	Class Names and Ages	Emblems or Symbols
December 1928	Names for Group 3, ages 8-9, to be Zeebees and Zeegees (Zion's Boys and Zion's Girls).	Red shield with white "Z" and "B" or "G" on it.
August, September 1929	*Groups:* (Boys and girls together in first 4 groups.) Beginners: Preschool age. Group 1: 6 years or Grade 1. Group 2: 7 years or Grade 2.	
	Group 3: 8 years or Grade 3. (Zebees & Zegees) *Boys' Groups — Trail Builders:* Blazers: 9 years or Grade 4.	See above (December 1928). Pine tree. Hatchet.
	Trekkers: 10 years or Grade 5.	Wheel.
	Guides: 11 years or Grade 6. *Girls' Groups — Home Builders:* Larks: 9 years or Grade 4.	Arrow. (1930.) Girl with lighted candle.
	Bluebirds: 10 years or Grade 5.	Bluebird in flight.
	Seagulls: 11 years or Grade 6.	Seagull in flight.

Colors	Mottoes or Codes	
Red for courage and white for purity.	"Be honest."	
	"Little builders, build away! Little builders, build today! Build a tower pure and bright, Build it up in deeds of light."	
See above (December 1928).	See above (December 1928).	
Green and brown.	"I'll strive to do my best to: Reverence my Heavenly Father in word and in deed, Be loyal to my Country, Honor my father and mother, Do a good turn daily." (1930.)	
Yellow and brown.	"Love Lights the Way."	
Blue and white.	"The World Needs Happiness Makers." (1930.)	
Silver or white plus background color.	"Serve Gladly."	

205

Years	Class Names and Ages	Emblems or Symbols
	Mi-kan-wees: 12-13 years or Grades 7 and 8 (public school grades). Mi-kan-wees discontinued in 1934 when girls 12-13 went into YWMIA.	Teepee, meaning home.
July 1940	Primary Seal appeared for first time on cover of *Children's Friend*, July 1940.	On the seal are the words: "Faith and Service—The Primary Association—Organized 1878—Church of Jesus Christ of Latter-day Saints."
1940-1942	*The Youngest Groups:* Group 1: 4 and 5 years. Group 2: 6 years.	
	Intermediate Groups: Zion's Boys & Girls First yr.: 7 years. Second yr.: 8 years.	Replica of boy's head and girl's head with "Zion's Boy" (or girl) and letters "L.D.S." in white on red felt shield, 1940. In 1942 another change in the shield was made. The boy and girl were both on one shield with words "Zion's Boys and Girls."
	Boys' Groups—Trail Builders (Same as 1930 except as noted.)	Cap design and motif changed.
	Girls' Groups—Home Builders: (same as 1930 except as noted.)	Home Builder emblem introduced, 1942: Home with girl in front of it.
	Larks	Picture of a lark replaced candle as Lark class emblem.

206

Colors	Mottoes or Codes	
Dark blue on white.	"Grow Better Every Day."	

The Primary colors: red, yellow, and blue— red for bravery, courage, fearless- ness; yellow for service; blue for truth, purity, and the clean life.	"Faith in God
	Service to
	  Our Fellowmen
	  Our Homes
	  Our Church
	  and Our Country."	

Red and white. Green and white for first year, 1942. Red and white for second year, 1942. Green for growth, red for courage and valor, white for purity. Green and orange.	"My shield is courage to be pure in heart." (Both years until fall 1942; second year motto after that.) First year motto, fall 1942: "As I grow I will keep my heart pure."	
	"By my daily conduct—both in word and in deed—I will show That I love my Father in heaven That I honor my parents That I am loyal to my country That I light the way with love." (Larks.) That I am a happiness maker." (Bluebirds.) That I serve gladly." (Seagulls.) (1942.)	

Years	Class Names and Ages	Emblems or Symbols
1948	*Boys' Groups—Trail Builders:* (Change in code to indicate progress in the three classes in Trail Building.)	
1949	*Girls' Groups—Home Builders:*	New Home Builder Emblem and code. Different drawings of birds for each group and new Lark and Bluebird mottoes.
	Larks: 9 years. Bluebirds: 10 years. Seagulls: 11 years.	Meadow lark. Bluebird. Seagull.
1951-1952	Following class changes made: Nursery Class: Under 4 years. Beginners: 4 years. Group 1: 5 years. Group 2: 6 years. Co-Pilots: 7 years.	Compass. (Letters RW mean "Right Way," and the compass represents the teachings of the Church.)
1953	Top-Pilots: 8 years.	Beacon. (Symbol of the truths Jesus taught, which will illuminate the children's pathway.)
1953	Cub Scout program and Scouting for boys 11 years assigned to Primary by the First Presidency. Guide Scout patrols replaced the Guide groups. Cub dens and packs organized.	
1956-1958	Name "Younger Groups" changed to *Junior Groups:* Nursery Class: 3 years.	

Colors	Mottoes or Codes	
	"I will strive to do my best in word and deed to Worship my Heavenly Father Be loyal to my country Honor my father and mother Blaze my trails cheerfully." (Blazer.) Trek forward bravely." (Trekker.) Guide with kindness." (Guide.)	
Yellow and brown. Blue and white. Silver or white plus one other color.	"I will strive to do my best, in word and deed, to Worship my Heavenly Father Be loyal to my country, Honor my father and mother, Greet the day with a song." (Larks.) Make others happy." (Bluebirds.) Serve gladly." (Seagulls.)	
	No motto given, but the idea is that "The Church of Jesus Christ of Latter-day Saints, like a compass, is a guide helping boys and girls find the Right Way." (Manual, 1952.)	
	"'I am the light of the world: he that followeth me shall not walk in darkness, but shall have the light of life.' I will try to follow him."	
	Note: When no motto or code was given for the younger classes following, a theme selected from the "Foreword" in the lesson manual has been used.	

Years	Class Names and Ages	Emblems or Symbols
	Sunbeams: 4 years.	
	Stars: 5 years.	Star (five points of star represent the five years of child's life).
	Rainbows: 6 years.	Rainbow has religious significance—"symbolizes the promise our Heavenly Father gave to Noah."
1959-1961	Name "Home Builders" changed to *Lihomas* (means "little homemakers"):	A home.
	Gaynotes: 9 years.	Musical "note" is challenge for each girl to improve her attitude, radiate happiness, and greet each day with a song.
	Firelights: 10 years.	Hearth with fire burning in it.
	Merrihands: 11 years.	Girl's hands holding the New Testament.
1959-1961	Trail Builders (Blazers, Trekkers, Guide Patrol) to have mural, "Trail to the Priesthood," to help prepare them for receiving the priesthood.	Pine tree. Hatchet (Blazers). Wheel (Trekkers). Arrow (Guide Patrol).
1961-1962	Name "Junior" for younger groups changed to *Skylets:* Nursery class became Moonbeams: 3 years.	

210

Colors	Mottoes or Codes	
Colors of the rainbow.	Name chosen because four-year-olds "give a sparkle of light and warmth to the world about them." Primary Stars "by their example will guide their associates to a better way of life." The rainbow "is meant to inspire the child to be a promise-keeper, too." "I will bring the light of the gospel into my home By greeting the day with a song." "I will bring the light of the gospel into my home By greeting the day with a song, By giving joy to others." "I will bring the light of the gospel into my home By greeting the day with a song, By giving joy to others, By serving gladly." "I will worship my Heavenly Father and grow in knowledge along my Trail to the Priesthood." Lesson titles all begin with "Our Heavenly Father Loves Us."	

Years	Class Names and Ages	Emblems or Symbols
1964-1966	Sunbeams: 4 years. (New manual, 1964.)	
	CTR Pilots: 6 years.	Plane wings with CTR on them.
	Right Way Pilots: 7 years.	Circle with "Right Way Pilots" inside and wings on sides.
1970-1978	Group names, Skylets, Pilots, Trail Builders, Lihomas eliminated. Classes structured as follows:	
	Moonbeams (1970): 3 years.	
	Sunbeams (1971): 3 years.	Sun.
	Stars A: 4 years. Stars B: 5 years.	Star.
	CTR A: 6 years. CTR B: 7 years.	"CTR" in white on green shield to remind child that the meaning of these letters will shield him from making wrong decisions.
	Targeteers A: 8 years. Targeteers B: 9 years. (Boys and girls in classes above.)	An arrow aiming at a target.
	Merrie Miss A: 10 years. Merrie Miss B: 11 years.	The lighted hearth.

Colors	*Mottoes or Codes*	
	Lesson titles begin with "Our Heavenly Father Loves Us."	
	"Choose the Right."	
	Symbolism of pilots and planes used to capture children's interest and enthusiasm "to live the right way by following the teachings of the gospel of Jesus Christ."	
	"A Sunbeam truly gives light and life to the world." He learns "that our Heavenly Father shows his love for us."	
Red star on white.	"When I am kind and when I obey, I give the world a happier day." (From "Star Song," Manual, 1970.)	
Green and white.	"Choose the Right."	
Red, yellow, blue.	"I aim to live the teachings of Jesus Christ."	
	"I will radiate the light of the gospel."	

Years	Class Names and Ages	Emblems or Symbols
	Blazer A: 10 years. Blazer B (Scouts): 11 years.	Lighted torch.

Colors	Mottoes or Codes	
	"I will prepare to receive and to honor the priesthood."	

Notes

Preface

[1] *Woman's Exponent* 10 (January 15, 1882): 128.

[2] Fine Arts Study Group, *Mountains Conquered, The Story of Morgan* (Morgan, Utah: Morgan County News Publishers, 1959), p. 326.

[3] *Journal of Discourses* 9:38-39.

[4] *Journal of Discourses* 15:11-12.

[5] Cache Valley Stake Relief Society Minute Book B, 1881-1914, October 20, 1890, p. 90, Church Archives, Historical Department of The Church of Jesus Christ of Latter-day Saints, Salt Lake City, Utah, hereinafter cited as Church Archives.

[6] "Woman and Her Duties," *Woman's Exponent* 8 (February 15, 1880): 140.

[7] "Be Valiant for Right," *Woman's Exponent* 37 (October 1908): 20.

[8] *Deseret News*, February 11, 1874.

[9] *Woman's Exponent* 2 (November 15, 1873): 94.

[10] Ibid., 2 (January 15, 1879): 125.

[11] "Early Education," *Woman's Exponent* 8 (June 15, 1879): 12.

[12] *Woman's Exponent* 2 (September 15, 1873): 62.

[13] Ellis Shipp Musser, ed., *The Early Autobiography and Diary of Ellis Reynolds Shipp* (Salt Lake City: Deseret News Press, 1962), p. 185.

[14] The work of the midwife was not restricted to assisting in childbirth or helping children. She often performed all of the medical functions in her community in the absence of a doctor.

[15] Journal of Discourses 26:100-101.

Chapter One: "Could There Not Be An Organization?"

[1] Aurelia Spencer Rogers, *Life Sketches of Orson Spencer and Others, and History of Primary Work* (Salt Lake City: George Q. Cannon & Sons, 1898), p. 208.

[2] Ibid., pp. 179-80.

[3] *Juvenile Instructor* 1 (May 1, 1866): 34.

[4] *Juvenile Instructor* 8 (June 7, 1873): 96.

[5] Ibid., pp. 205-6.

[6] *Woman's Exponent* 6 (February 15, 1878): 138.

[7] Eliza R. Snow Smith, "Sketch of My Life," p. 39, microfilm of holograph, Church Archives; original in Bancroft Library, University of California, Berkeley, California.

[8] *Life Sketches*, p. 209.

[9] Ibid., pp. 209-10.

[10] Ibid., p. 212.

[11] Farmington Ward, Davis Stake, Primary Association Minutes, August 11, 1878, p. 2, Church Archives.

[12] Ibid., p. 3.

[13] *Woman's Exponent* 7 (September 1, 1878): 53.

[14] *Life Sketches*, pp. 261-63.

[15] *Woman's Exponent* 7 (September 1, 1878): 54.

[16] *Woman's Exponent* 7 (October 1, 1878): 66.

[17] Hyrum Ward, Cache Stake, Relief Society Minutes, 1870-79, September 2, 1869, p. 81, Church Archives.

[18] *Woman's Exponent* 10 (March 1, 1882): 151.

[19]Violet Lunt Urie, "Autobiography," photocopy, Church Archives.

[20]*Juvenile Instructor* 28 (May 1, 1893): 201.

[21]Farmington Ward Primary Minutes, December 7, 1878, pp. 12-13.

[22]*Woman's Exponent* 8 (December 1, 1879): 110.

Chapter Two: "Worthy of All Honor"

[1]Eliza R. Snow to Robert Welch, December 25, 1881, holograph, Church Archives.

[2]St. George First Ward, St. George Stake, Primary Association Minutes, 1880-1886, pp. 1-3, Church Archives.

[3]*Woman's Exponent* 12 (April 15, 1884): 175.

[4]Eliza R. Snow, *Bible Questions and Answers for Children* (Salt Lake City: Juvenile Instructor Office, 1881), p. 33.

[5]Eliza R. Snow, *Recitations for the Primary Associations in Poetry, Dialogue, and Prose, Book No. 1* (Salt Lake City: Deseret News Co., 1881), p. 68.

[6]*Jubilee History of Latter-day Saints Sunday Schools* (Salt Lake City: Deseret Sunday School Union, 1900), pp. 24-25.

[7]"Home Affairs," *Woman's Exponent* 8 (January 15, 1880): 124.

[8]*Woman's Exponent* 12 (August 15, 1883): 42.

[9]*Woman's Exponent* 13 (January 1, 1885): 119.

[10]Kate B. Carter, ed., "The Primary Association," *Our Pioneer Heritage*, 20 vols. (Salt Lake City: Daughters of Utah Pioneers, 1972), 15:162-63.

[11]*Woman's Exponent* 13 (April 15, 1885): 173.

[12]"Home Affairs," *Woman's Exponent* 11 (January 15, 1883): 124.

[13]*Woman's Exponent* 12 (April 15, 1884): 175.

[14]*Woman's Exponent* 11 (September 1, 1882): 54.

[15]*Woman's Exponent* 12 (November 15, 1883): 91.

[16]Rogers, *Life Sketches,* pp. 227-28.

[17]"The Primary Association," in Carter, *Our Pioneer Heritage* 15:175.

[18]*Woman's Exponent* 10 (November 1, 1881): 86.

[19]*Woman's Exponent* 7 (May 1, 1879): 238.

[20]Goshen Ward, Santaquin-Tintic Stake, Primary Association Minutes, 1878-1882, April 21, 1879, p. 17, Church Archives.

[21]Eighth Ward, Liberty Stake, Relief Society Minutes, 1874-1882, December 2, 1880, Church Archives.

[22]Seventeenth Ward, Salt Lake Stake, Relief Society Minutes, 1871-1884, January [21?] and February 4, 1880, Church Archives.

[23]*Woman's Exponent* 9 (August 1, 1880): 37.

[24]"The Primary Association," in Carter, *Our Pioneer Heritage* 15:177-78.

[25]Ibid., p. 178.

[26]*Woman's Exponent* 13 (December 15, 1884): 111.

[27]LaVern Watts Parmley Papers, Church Archives.

[28]Rogers, *Life Sketches,* p. 227.

[29]Ibid., pp. 222-23.

[30]Journal History of the Church, April 21, 1928, p. 4, Church Archives.

[31]Ibid.

[32]"L. B. Felt's History," n.p., holograph, Church Archives.

[33]*Woman's Exponent* 9 (July 1, 1880): 21-22.

[34]Lillie Tuckett Freeze, "Primary Work from 1880-1890," p. 2, holograph, Church Archives.

[35]Lillie Tuckett Freeze, "A Bit of History Prior to 1880," p. 3, holograph, Church Archives.

[36]Freeze, "Primary Work," p. 4.

Chapter Three: Taking the Helm

[1]Primary General Board Minutes,

1889-1901, October 3, 1889, p. 3, Church Archives.

[2]Ibid., October 3, 1890, p. 4.

[3]Ibid., p. 24.

[4]Primary General Board Minutes, 1899-1903, November 26, 1899, p. 5.

[5]Goshen Ward, Santaquin-Tintic Stake, Primary Minutes, 1878-1882, March 29, 1879, p. 14, Church Archives.

[6]Primary General Board Minutes, October 5, 1896, p. 24.

[7]"Mary and May," *Children's Friend* 18 (December 1919): 421-22.

[8]Lillie T. Freeze, "Primary Work from 1880-1890."

[9]Journal History, June 9, 1934, p. 7.

[10]*Deseret Evening News,* December 24, 1895, p. 8.

[11]Reminiscence of Mrs. Wm. Stewart, Marie Fox Felt Collection, Marriott Library, University of Utah, Salt Lake City, Utah.

[12]Freeze, "Primary Work," p. 3.

[13]Primary General Board Minutes, 1889-1901, October 5, 1896, pp. 24-25.

[14]Ibid., April 6, 1896, pp. 17-18.

[15]Ibid., April 9, 1898, p. 33.

[16]Rogers, *Life Sketches,* p. 328. See also Primary Board Minutes, July 4, 1897, p. 31.

[17]*Woman's Exponent* 29 (January 1:1901): 69-70.

[18]*Children's Friend* 11 (January 1912): 38.

[19]Relief Society General Board Minutes, 1842-44 and 1872-1915, October 3, 1896, p. 163, Church Archives.

[20]Primary General Board Minutes, 1899-1903, April 6, 1910, p. 49.

[21]Belle S. Spafford, Oral History Interview by Jill Mulvay Derr, 1975-76, p. 109, Church Archives.

[22]Primary General Board Minutes, 1899-1903, April 6, 1901, p. 49.

[23]See Allan Dean Payne, "The Mormon Response to Early Progressive Education, 1892-1920" (Ph.D. diss., University of Utah, 1977); and John S. McCormick, "The Primary Association, 1902-1952," Ms, History Division, Church Archives.

[24]Primary General Board Minutes, 1905-1908, November 23, 1906, p. 117.

[25]*Children's Friend* 1 (January 1902): 4.

[26]*Children's Friend* 7 (January 1908): 26.

Chapter Four: "For the Betterment of Children"

[1]"The Primary Teachers Class," *Children's Friend* 12 (August 1913): 457.

[2]Ibid., p. 453.

[3]*Children's Friend* 12 (April 1913): 215.

[4]Ibid.

[5]Ibid., p. 217.

[6]Lillie T. Freeze, "The First Primary Teachers' Class," *Children's Friend* 12 (July 1913): 391.

[7]*Children's Friend* 12 (April 1913): 193.

[8]*Children's Friend* 6 (March 1907): 123.

[9]Correlation Committee, Minutes, 1913-1920, p. 3, Church Archives.

[10]Ibid., pp. 16-17.

[11]Joint Correlation-Social Advisory Committee, Minutes, 1920-1922, April 12, 1921, Church Archives.

[12]*Children's Friend* 13 (January 1914): 39.

[13]Ibid.

[14]Primary General Board Minutes, 1911-1918, July 13, 1917, p. 318.

[15]*Children's Friend* 17 (November 1918): 433.

[16]*Children's Friend* 17 (April 1918): 153.

[17]Ibid., pp. 181-85.

[18]*Relief Society Magazine* 4 (January 1917): 36-38.

[19]Social Advisory Committee, Minutes, 1916-1920, July 9, 1918, Church Archives.

[20]Ibid., May 6, 1919.

[21]Ibid., October 4, 1919.

[22]*Children's Friend* 21 (August 1922): 425.

[23]*The Primary Children's Hospital,* pamphlet (Primary Association, 1950), Church Archives.

[24]Primary General Board Minutes, 1920-1924, February 8, 1922, p. 119.

[25]*Children's Friend* 23 (June 1924): 167-69.

[26]*Children's Friend* 24 (May 1925): 182.

[27]Primary General Board Minutes,

1920-1924, October 19, 1921, pp. 97-98.

[28]Primary General Board Minutes, 1918-1920, April 12, 1918, p. 14.

[29]Journal History of the Church, June 9, 1934, pp. 5-7.

[30]May Anderson to Lillie Tuckett Freeze, May 9, 1917, holograph, Church Archives.

[31]Louie B. Felt to Lillie Tuckett Freeze, May 8, 1917, holograph, Church Archives.

[32]Primary General Board Minutes, 1920-1924, February 21, 1923, p. 207, Church Archives.

[33]Lillie T. Freeze, "History Prior to 1880," p. 4.

Chapter Five: The Primary Comes of Age

[1]*Children's Friend* 27 (July 1928): 268.

[2]Ibid., p. 265.

[3]Ibid., p. 266.

[4]*Woman's Exponent* 12 (November 1, 1883): 86.

[5]*Children's Friend* 20 (September 1921): 350-57. See also *Millennial Star* 82 (August 5, 1920): 511; 83 (March 24, 1921): 192; 83 (October 13, 1921): 652.

[6]*Children's Friend* 28 (February 1929): 73. See also *Millennial Star* 90 (October 25, 1928): 677-79.

[7]Ibid.

[8]*Millennial Star* 92 (November 27, 1920): 827-29.

[9]Primary General Board Minutes, 1920-1924, April 9, 1924, pp. 282-86.

[10]Ibid.

[11]*Millennial Star* 92 (November 27, 1920): 824.

[12]Report of Conferences of the Presidents of the European Missions, 1936, 1937, and 1938, in Amy Brown Lyman Collection, Church Archives.

[13]Ibid. (French Mission, 1938).

[14]Ibid. (Swedish Mission, 1938).

[15]Primary General Board Minutes, 1920-1924, October 26, 1921, p. 99.

[16]Copies of letters are included in Primary General Board Minutes, 1928-1933, October 1, 1930, p. 110, and January 7, 1931, p. 122.

[17]*A Handbook for Officers and Teachers in the Primary Association (Religion Class)*, (Salt Lake City: General Board of Primary Associations, 1930), p. 39.

[18]Ibid., p. 78.

[19]Primary General Board Minutes, 1928-1933, April 12, 1933, p. 260.

[20]Primary General Board Minutes, 1933-1940, August 15, 1934, p. 325.

[21]Ibid., July 23, 1934, p. 324.

[22]*Children's Friend* 51 (February 1952): 76.

[23]*Handbook*, foreword.

[24]Primary General Board Minutes, 1928-1933, June 15, 1932, p. 215.

[25]Ibid., p. 217.

[26]Primary General Board Minutes, 1933-1940, August 22, 1939, p. 601.

[27]Ibid., September 21, 1939, p. 607.

[28]Ibid., December 19, 1939, pp. 624-25.

[29]Frances Grant Bennett, *Glimpses of a Mormon Family* (Salt Lake City: Deseret Book, 1968), p. 177.

[30]Lowell Bennion to May Anderson, May 12, 1943, holograph, Church Archives.

Chapter Six: The Transition Years

[1]Ruth Hinckley Willes, ed., "Autobiography of Bryant S. Hinckley," 1971, p. 45, Church Archives.

[2]At the time Sister Hinckley took office, the executive officers of the Primary were referred to as the superintendent and assistants. Sister Hinckley requested permission of the First Presidency of the Church to change the titles to president and counselors, which was granted in April 1942. See Minutes of the General Board of Primary Association, 1940-1947, April 9, 1942, p. 119, Church Archives.

[3]Willes, p. 47.

[4]Adele Cannon Howells Diary, January 19, 1940, Church Archives.

[5]Primary Association General Board

Minutes, 1940-1947, January 15, 1941, p. 59.

[6]*A Handbook for the Officers and Teachers in the Primary Association, Church of Jesus Christ of Latter-day Saints* (Salt Lake City: The General Board of Primary Associations, 1930), p. 105.

[7]Primary Association General Board Minutes, 1940-1947, January 23, 1940, p. 1.

[8]Ibid., February 14, 1940, p. 6.

[9]Ibid.

[10]*Deseret News,* November 2, 1940.

[11]Primary Association General Board Minutes, 1940-1947, July 17, 1940, p. 34.

[12]Ibid., April 17, 1941, p. 70.

[13]Fairbanks Branch, Alaskan-Canadian Mission, Primary Association Minutes, 1941-1952, 1954-1955, June 3, 1941, p. 4; September 9, 1950, p. 58; January 8, 1955, p. 34, Church Archives.

[14]Adele Cannon Howells Diary, January 14, 1944; February 10, 1944.

[15]Ibid., October 29, 1942; *Primary Handbook,* 1930, p. 105.

[16]*Children's Friend* 40 (October 1941): 456-57.

[17]Relief Society Magazine 30 (June-July 1943): 377.

Chapter Seven: Expanding Horizons

[1]*Salt Lake Telegram,* July 18, 1947.

[2]Adele Cannon Howells Diary, August 14, 1943, Church Archives.

[3]*Young Woman's Journal* 24 (August 1913): 463-69.

[4]Howells Diary, March 10, 1950; July 26, 1950.

[5]Mary Pratt Parrish, Oral History, interviews by Gordon Irving, 1973, pp. 44-46, Church Archives.

[6]*Teacher Training Lessons* (Salt Lake City: The General Board of the Primary Association, 1950), p. 5.

[7]*Children's Friend* 47 (November 1948): 498.

[8]Primary Association General Board Minutes, 1947-1949, March 31, 1949, p. 119.

[9]Anna Rosenkilde to President Heber

J. Grant, November 6, 1937, Church Archives.

[10]Church Section, *Deseret News,* February 25, 1956.

[11]*Children's Friend* 49 (January 1950): 32.

[12]Frances G. Bennett, *Glimpses of a Mormon Family* (Salt Lake City: Deseret Book Company, 1968), p. 182.

[13]Catharine A. Rich, et al., compilers, *The Primary Children's Hospital* (Salt Lake City: Deseret Book, 1967), p. 6.

[14]*Salt Lake Telegram,* July 18, 1947.

[15]Parrish, p. 49.

[16]Howells Diary, January 29, 1950.

Chapter Eight: "Going Up Against a Stone Wall"

[1]Adele Cannon Howells Diary, January 23, 1950, Church Archives.

[2]LaVern Watts Parmley, Oral History, interviews by Jill Mulvay Derr, 1974-1976, p. 11, Church Archives.

[3]*Cub Scouting in the Church of Jesus Christ of Latter-day Saints* (Salt Lake City: The General Board of the Primary Association, 1963), p. 12.

[4]Parmley, p. 53.

[5]First Presidency to General Board of the Primary Association, May 28, 1952, Church Archives.

[6]*Cub Scouting in the Church of Jesus Christ of Latter-day Saints* (Salt Lake City: The Church of Jesus Christ of Latter-day Saints, 1978), p. 9.

[7]Parmley, p. 149.

[8]Ibid., pp. 134, 146.

[9]Ibid., p. 148.

[10]Ibid., p. 149.

[11]*Deseret Sunday School Songs,* 1909, p. 114.

[12]Jane Hooper Blood Diary, postscript, p. 6, typescript copy of excerpts in possession of author.

[13]*Sing With Me,* no. B-76, and Church News, *Deseret News,* April 1, 1978.

[14]*Inservice Manual* (Salt Lake City:

The General Board of the Primary Association, 1953), p. 3.

[15]Mary Parrish Oral History, p. 51.

[16]Parmley, p. 29.

[17]Ibid., p. 34.

Chapter Nine: "A Difference Almost Miraculous"

[1]*Woman's Exponent* 13 (December 15, 1884): 111.

[2]Goshen Ward, Santaquin-Tintic Stake Primary Association Minutes, 1878-1882, March 29, 1879, p. 14, Church Archives.

[3]Primary Association General Board Minutes, 1952-1955, January 27, 1955, p. 731, Church Archives.

[4]Ibid., February 10-17, 1955, p. 737.

[5]LaVern Watts Parmley, Oral History, interviews by Jill Mulvay Derr, 1974-1976, pp. 124-25.

[6]"Primary Script," vol. 12, no. 3 (1967-68), p. 3.

[7]Personal papers of Ada S. Van Dam, former Primary general board member, Salt Lake City, Utah.

[8]Ibid.

[9]Interview with Lois C. Sprunt, Primary general board member, October 1977.

[10]Parmley, p. 150.

[11]*Children's Friend* 53 (July 1954): 294.

[12]Parmley, p. 151.

[13]Primary Association General Board Minutes, February 9, 1961, p. 4008.

[14]*Improvement Era* 73 (December 1970): 12.

[15]Parmley, p. 82.

[16]In Catharine A. Rich, et al., compilers, *The Primary Children's Hospital* (Salt Lake City: Deseret Book, 1967), p. 7.

[17]Parmley, p. 82.

[18]Ibid., p. 77.

[19]Ibid., p. 98.

[20]By Irene Christopherson, in *The Primary Song Book* (Salt Lake City: The General Board of the Primary Association, 1939), p. 160.

[21]Parmley, p. 32.

[22]Ibid., p. 33.

[23]Ibid., p. 103.

Chapter Ten: "I Love Primary"

[1]"Primary Script," vol. 15, no. 3 (1970-71), p. 5.

[2]Marion G. Romney, Primary Conference address, April 1949.

[3]Jeanine W. Marichal to Trilba J. Lindsay, Primary general board member, December 11, 1972.

[4]Marichal to Lindsay, February 4, 1974.

[5]Cache Stake Primary Minute Book A, 1882-1912, October 24, 1885, p. 28, Church Archives.

[6]Salt Lake Stake Relief Society Conference Minutes, 1880-1896, September 17, 1882, p. 33, Church Archives.

[7]Marichal to Lindsay, July 27, 1975.

[8]Ibid., March 7, 1973.

[9]Kikue Matsui to Dwan J. Young, Primary general board member, February 7, 1978.

[10]Kyoko Toyama to Dwan J. Young, December 1977.

[11]Primary Conference address, June 17, 1947.

[12]*Ensign* 8 (April 1978): 23.

[13]*Woman's Exponent* 17 (March 1, 1889): 146.

[14]Jane Hooper Blood Diary, May 2, 1894, typescript copy of excerpts in possession of author.

[15]Ina Hatch Parkinson, "Sketch of Ruth A. Hatch Hale," from the papers of Blanche Hatch Woodland in S. George Ellsworth, "An Inventory of Historical Resource Materials for Cache Valley," Utah-Idaho (Logan, 1947), microfilm copy, Church Archives.

[16]Kate B. Carter, ed., "The Primary Association," *Our Pioneer Heritage* (Salt Lake City: Daughters of the Utah Pioneers, 1972), p. 177.

[17]*Woman's Exponent* 10 (August 15, 1881): 48.

[18]Letter to Dwan J. Young, December 1977.

[19]Spencer W. Kimball, Primary Conference address, April 1949.

[20]*Journal of Discourses:* 26:100-101.

Index